THE FELLOWSHIP
OF THE
HOLY SPIRIT

Dana Congdon

ISBN: 978-1-942521-57-0

Available from:

Christian Testimony Ministry
4424 Huguenot Road
Richmond, Virginia 23235

www.christiantestimonyministry.com

Printed in USA

CONTENTS

THE PERSON OF THE HOLY SPIRIT

John 14:1-3—Let not your heart be troubled; [you] believe in God, believe also in Me. In My Father's house are many [abiding] places; if it were not so, I would have told you; for I go to prepare a place for you. And if I go and prepare a place for you, I will come again, and receive you to Myself; that where I am, there you may be also.

John 14:16-23—And I will ask the Father, and He will give you another [Comforter], that He may be with you forever; that is the Spirit of truth, whom the world cannot receive, because it does not behold Him or know Him, but you know Him because He abides with you, and will be in you. I will not leave you as orphans; I will come to you. After a little while the world will behold Me no more; but you will behold Me; because I live, you shall live also. In that day you shall know that I am in My Father, and you in Me, and I in you. He who has My commandments and keeps them, he it is who loves Me; and he who loves Me shall be loved by My Father, and I will love him, and will disclose Myself to him. Judas (not Iscariot) said to Him, "Lord, what then has happened that You are going to disclose Yourself to us, and not to the world?" Jesus answered and said to him, "If anyone loves Me, he will keep My word; and My Father will love him, and We will come to him, and make Our abode with him.

II Corinthians 13:14—The grace of the Lord Jesus Christ, and the love of God, and the fellowship of the Holy Spirit, be with you all.

Father, we come to You again, thanking You for Your living word, realizing that it becomes living to us through the breathing of the Holy Spirit upon Your word. How You love Your word and, Lord, we cherish it too. We thank you for the ministries, even in these last days, of encouragement regarding the studying of the word of God.

Now, as we come, we come needing even this One we come to talk about. Please, Holy Spirit, come down upon us and give us life and quickening, revelation and understanding, truth and freedom. We gather together in the name of Jesus, casting our eyes toward Him, thanking You for this precious benediction we have. In the name of Jesus Christ our Lord. Amen.

We are not here to gain more knowledge but to dwell in an abiding place that has been provided for us. We read about this in John 14, that the Father has a house for us and we are part of His household. We have gained entrance into that family through Jesus Christ and His amazing grace. Now we stand in that grace through faith in Jesus Christ, and as we live our lives in this blessed benediction we sense the wonderful and loving steward, the Holy Spirit, ministering the things of Christ to us. This benediction we have before us in II Corinthians is a blessedness. It is more than knowledge; it is a place to live. Because the apostle Paul had been through the cross, through resurrection, through the dealing of the Holy Spirit, through the grace of the Lord Jesus, and knew the love of God, by the end of II Corinthians, after sharing his heart, he realizes that the end of it all is for us to be able to abide in this place—in the grace of our Lord Jesus Christ, and the love of God, and in the fellowship of the Holy Spirit. Paul was a spiritual man, as much as any man can be upon this earth, and he abode in the vortex of that reality, living in the good of it, in the full salvation.

LIVING IN THE HOUSE OF GOD

Sometimes, when we sing choruses and songs, I think to myself, "If I could only live in what I am singing." We sing words of love and adoration and giving our whole lives to God. I wish that it were so, and by the grace of God, may it be one day that we will not be so far behind the words that we speak. When we see the benediction in II Corinthians, we realize this is a place to dwell. Oh, that we could live in the good of our salvation, really living in the grace of the Lord Jesus Christ, experiencing the love of God, and being found in the communion of the Holy Spirit; but in fact, we often find that our experience is occasional visits to this place. This is a blessedness for us, a wonderful place; it is the Father's house. That is where His love is to us.

I thank God through Jesus Christ that when I was 20 years old I got saved by His amazing grace and found myself in a household—in the house of God. What a wonderful thing to abide in the household of God. It is better than Psalm 133 where we have the occasional feast and we sense that it is such a blessed thing for brethren to dwell together in unity. But the Lord commands the blessing all the time in His house. Every time we gather around His table, it is not just an annual feast. It is better than the cleft in Mount Sinai where you can see a little bit of the glory. We can behold Jesus' face from glory to glory because of His grace. It is ours to enjoy. We have such a place to live, and we need to live there. It is by the precious ministry of the Holy Spirit, as He deals with us and leads us, that we find ourselves abiding there.

Don't think Paul was any different from the rest of us. When he was first saved, he longed to dwell in the house of the Lord but found himself sometimes in and sometimes out, sometimes struggling with sin and feeling condemned because he was out, and then the grace of God ministered to him again and he was back inside. Would it not be wonderful to live under the revelation of what has been shared about the grace of the Lord Jesus. What a precious love, what a wonderful grace the Lord ministered to the woman at the well and other various stories in the gospel of John. The Lord wants us to live there, and Paul comes to the end of it all after dealing with the Corinthians, sometimes very harshly, and he says (in my words), "I just want you to know that there is a house that you can live in because the Father loves you, and by the grace of the Lord Jesus you have been given the door in. He is the foundation. By the communion of the Holy Spirit you can stay there and see all the riches of Christ and enter into the good of all your inheritance in Jesus. I am correcting you, I am adjusting you, I am speaking to you, I am sharing my heart with you in all of this so that we can dwell forever in the house of the Lord all the days of our lives." So this is a benediction for us to enter into.

WHO IS THE HOLY SPIRIT?

If we want to enter into the communion of the Holy Spirit, of course, it necessitates us knowing who the Holy Spirit is. So I want to touch on this matter of the Person of the Holy Spirit. strange to say, even though the Holy Spirit has come into our lives from the moment of our salvation and He has worked with us, He has been patient with us, He has spoken to us, He has comforted and healed us, yet in a strange sort of way, He is not known by Christians. We have His acquaintance, and we see clues of His life, but to know the Holy Spirit is to be able to commune with the Holy Spirit.

Within the Godhead, it is true, the Holy Spirit presents a problem to us in our understanding of who He is. The Father and the Son are ready analogies for us. We understand what Father is and we understand what Son is, but what is a Spirit? The Bible says you must always keep in mind that the Spirit is wind and breath. That is an analogy for us but it is not like Father and Son. So we say, "Who is the Holy Spirit?" He is wind and breath. Does that help you very much? Of course, He is a Person, but the Hebrew word *ruah* means wind or breath. So it can be used spirit, wind or breath, depending on the context in the Old Testament. In the New Testament, the word *pneuma* also means wind, breath or spirit, depending on the context. You will have to figure it out, but the point is that we should never get too far away from this understanding of the

Spirit. He is the very breath of God. You are only as dependent upon the Spirit as you are upon your own breath for life. He is the very wind of God, blowing, moving, shaping, and we need that wind.

Getting to know the Holy Spirit is not always so easy, and it is made more complicated by the fact that He will not show Himself to the natural man. It says in I Corinthians 2 that the things of the Spirit are foolishness to man. The natural man cannot understand this stuff. Then, in John 14 it says that the Holy Spirit cannot be received or beheld by the world. So, when you mention the Holy Spirit to somebody in the world, they think, "Oh boy, here we go, spooks, ghosts." They have no idea what is being shared. But the Christian should know unless we are using our natural mind to try to understand who the Holy Spirit is, which is possible because we have been so crammed with the knowledge of the world and the wisdom of the world in not understanding who the Spirit is. Often, we do not know Him as we think we do. So, the world cannot understand Him, but neither can we if we hold on to our misunderstandings or worldly understandings of Him.

THE HOLY SPIRIT STAYS IN THE BACKGROUND

Another problem happens when we become Christians in understanding the Holy Spirit. Through the ministry of the Holy Spirit we are born again; He regenerates us. Then, after we are born again, He, as it were, moves into the background and He holds up the Father for us. He convinces us, by speaking to our spirit, "You are a child of God, say 'Abba, Father.' He is your Father; you are connected. Get to know the Father, fellowship with the Father, and you can know the assurance of your salvation." Then the Spirit says, "Here is Jesus, and there is Jesus," and you open the Bible and He says, "There is Jesus"; but the Holy Spirit is sort of in the background. This is sometimes misunderstood as if the Holy Spirit is shy, personally, and a little bit reticent. He is the shy One of the Three. The other Two are talkative, but not this One; this One is shy. But I do not really believe this is true of who He is. There are some things we do not understand immediately about the nature of God

9

Himself but the Holy Spirit is very God, truly God. He is co-equal, co-eternal with the Father and the Son and He is not shy. But there is something in the nature of God that we saw in Jesus when He was on earth and it is also true of the Holy Spirit. In the Godhead, there is true deference which means a preferring of another more than ourselves. The Holy Spirit is not shy; neither is He trying to hide. He just prefers that you know the Father and the Son.

Even when Jesus was on earth, though He was in the form of God, He was not insecure about His need to be equal with God (see Philippians 2), neither is the Holy Spirit insecure about these things. But in true deference, He shows us the Father and He shows us the Son. I think if there is any sort of war in the heavens it is just over this: Who is going to show who-what between the Father, Son, and Holy Spirit; they love each other so. The only analogy that I know on this earth that I have ever seen is three Chinese Christian men fighting over who is going to pay for the dinner. They almost fight over who is going to pay the bill. Myself, being an American, I never get to pay. But between the

Father, Son and Holy Spirit, there is no feigned deference or cultural deference; it is true deference. It is the same kind that Paul exhorts us with when he tells us to prefer one another on the basis of this agape love.

But there is even more to it than that. It is not that the Holy Spirit is trying to hide from us. It is just that we also do not understand that when God does something, Father, Son, or Holy Spirit is focused and concentrated according to His purpose. The Holy Spirit has a purpose and He is concentrated on His purpose. He does not want things distracting. He does not want people to look at Him and say, "I will spend some time just worshiping You, Holy Spirit." He says, "Let's get down to business here. You need to be perfected in Christ." So we have a problem right from the start, if we could say a problem. The communion of the Holy Spirit is not for the purpose of His own self-disclosure. He has a purpose in this dispensation and until He gets the job done, He would rather defer any speculations, any thoughts about Him in order that we could look on the things that are important.

A few years ago this wonderful chorus was written that we all sang, "Father, we love You, we praise You, we adore You." Then we come to the third verse and, originally, it was "Spirit, we love You, we praise You, we adore You; glorify Thy name in all the earth," because it fit symmetrically with the other two verses about the Father and the Son. But one day, a worshiper, somebody sensitive to the Holy Spirit started singing it and when he came to the third verse, he started singing, "Spirit, we love You, we praise You, we adore You; glorify Thy name in all the earth," suddenly, the Spirit said, "No, I am not interested in glorifying My name in all the earth." And whoever it was said, "What should we say? Let's change the words." The one I like the best says, "Lead us to the Son and all His work." That is more according to His purpose. If you sing "Glorify Thy name in all the earth," the Holy Spirit says, "Not so, I am not interested right now. We have important things to do." He is concentrated on this wonderful purpose, so He defers and stands in the background in order to accomplish His purpose. I am fully persuaded that the Holy Spirit had a hand in the creation of the Apostles' Creed. It talks about the Father, it gives the different operations and descriptions of the Son and then in the Apostles' Creed it says, "I believe in the Holy Ghost." That is it! I think He had a hand in writing that. He is fellowshiping with a purpose.

THREE-WAY FELLOWSHIP

When we look at I John 1, we see a precious fellowship presented before us. There is a magnificent picture here of a three-way fellowship.

I John 1:1-4—What was from the beginning, what we have heard, what we have seen with our eyes, what we beheld and our hands handled, concerning the Word of Life—and the life was manifested, and we have seen and bear witness and proclaim to you the eternal life, which was with the Father and was manifested to us—what we have seen and heard we proclaim to you also, that you also may have fellowship with us; and indeed our fellowship is with the Father, and with His Son Jesus Christ. And these things we write, so that our joy may be made complete.

Here we see a blessed triangle of fellowship. Before the world ever was, there was fellowship between the Father and the Son. This is an eternal fellowship, a sharing of all things in common. The Father shared His life with the Son and the Son shared His life with the Father, and they communicated their life and their love and their truth back and forth, one to another, through eternity. This fellowship has always been. But then, wonderfully, miraculously, because Jesus came down and became the Word of Life in the flesh for us, died on the cross, rose again and saved us, we have entered into this fellowship. Can you imagine this? Here is the Father talking to the Son and the Son is talking to the Father, and now we are talking to the Father and talking to the Son and we are listening to the two talking to each other. In Isaiah 6, when he hears, probably, the Father and the Son saying, "Whom shall I send and who will go for Us?" we enter into this divine fellowship by the grace of our Lord Jesus Christ. But do you notice that there is nothing mentioned of the Spirit? Is He missing in this fellowship? No; we would never be in that fellowship if it were not for His quickening, born-again regeneration. We would never last in that fellowship if He were not continually keeping the lines of communication open by washing us in the precious blood of Jesus Christ, by washing us with the word of truth. So, even though His name is not mentioned, once again, behind the scenes, He is the very life being communicated between the Father and Son and us. He is in this fellowship but He is in the background and He is leading us to the Father and to the Son, and this is our communion with the Holy Spirit. He works intimately, He works hands on, His fellowship is very personal. So we find, once again, a problem, if we want to call it a problem; He is veiled within this very intimate work that He does. There is a three-fold veiling that makes seeing the Holy Spirit standing alone a bit difficult.

THE THREE-FOLD VEILING OF THE HOLY SPIRIT IN HIS WORK

Identified With the Lord Jesus

Number One: He is totally identified, at times, with the Lord Jesus Himself. They are one, after all, the Son and the Spirit, in such a way that there are moments in the Scriptures where the distinction seems to be blurred. I know that you come upon those Scriptures and you say to yourself: "Now, is that the Holy Spirit or is it Jesus?" I will point you to a few Scriptures, the ones that you especially know. In Philippians 1:19, He is called the Spirit of Jesus Christ. In Acts 16:6-7, as Paul began to go into Asia, the Holy Spirit prevented him from going that way; then, he started going another way and the Spirit of Jesus forbade him. Is that the same? It must be the same. Why does He say, "the Spirit of Jesus"? Sometimes, there is such an identity in their work and operation that it is not so clearly seen. In Romans 8:9-10, we also see a great unity between the two of them. "However, you are not in the flesh but in the Spirit, if indeed the Spirit of God dwells in you. But if anyone does not have the Spirit of Christ, he does not belong to Him. And if Christ is in you, though the body is dead because of sin, yet the spirit is alive because of righteousness."

Now who is in you? Is Christ in you? Is the Spirit in you? It is the Spirit of Christ and I am not sure that we will be able to clearly separate which is which.

In Galatians 4:6 it says, "And because you are sons, God has sent forth the Spirit of His Son into our hearts, crying, 'Abba! Father!" (Galatians 4:6) Of course, that is the Holy Spirit in our hearts crying, "Abba! Father!" But wait a minute, it is the Spirit of His Son. Don't forget that Jesus has a body, soul and spirit. Is it the Spirit of His Son that is in us crying "Abba!"? After all, He is the Son, He is the Father, He is saying "Abba." Is it Jesus saying "Abba"? Is it the Holy Spirit saying "Abba"? I am not sure we can really quite separate it or understand it.

In II Corinthians 3:16-18, we see that there is a switching of the definition of lordship in some sense that makes it a little unclear as to who, exactly, is being spoken of.

"But whenever a man turns to the Lord, the veil is taken away. (Now we know who that is. When you turn to the Lord Jesus, the veil is taken away.) Now the Lord is the Spirit; and where the Spirit of the Lord is, there is liberty. (Now that makes sense.) But we all, with unveiled face beholding as in a mirror the glory of the Lord (we know that is Jesus), are being transformed into the same image from glory to glory, just as from the Lord, the Spirit."

Even in the matter of lordship we will not be able to easily separate the difference between the Lord Jesus at times and the Spirit.

In John 14:16, Jesus said very clearly: "And I will ask the Father, and He will give you another Helper." Now we understand that Jesus is going and He is going to send another Helper, even the Spirit of truth. But then, immediately, verse 18 says, "I will not leave you as orphans; I will come to you." Does He mean now or later or when He is coming back the second time? No, it does not quite mean that.

Then verse 23 says, "Jesus answered and said to him, 'If anyone loves Me, he will keep My word; and My Father will love him, and We will come to him, and make Our abode with him.'" Who is abiding there, exactly—the Father, the Son, the Holy Spirit? Is it the Spirit or Jesus who has come back to abide in us?

Take verse 20 as an example: "In that day you shall know that I am in My Father." All right, we will draw some circles here. Here is the Father's circle and now Jesus is inside the circle. "I am in my Father and you are in Me," Now we are in Jesus, thank God for that, and then "and I am in you." The Holy Spirit identifies with the Lord Jesus in His ministry and His work and in His ministrations to us in such a way that, at times, it is hard to see the difference. But there are other Scriptures that make it clear that there is quite a distinction of the Persons, even the one we are studying: "The grace of our Lord Jesus, the love of God, the fellowship of the Holy Spirit." Or again in Revelation 22:17: "And the Spirit and the bride say, 'Maranatha'" to Jesus. There is a clear difference there.

Veiled In His Union With Our Human Spirit

The Holy Spirit is also veiled because of the nature of His very personal work. He is veiled in His unity of being indwelt in our human spirit. We have two words for *spirit.* Sometimes, it is the human spirit; sometimes, it is the Holy Spirit. If you are a translator of the Greek New

Testament, every letter in the original codices of the papyri are capital, upper case. When is Spirit capitalized and when is it small "s", human spirit? Sometimes the Holy Spirit is in such a union with our human spirit that it is a little hard to tell. Most of the contexts in the New Testament leaves you very clearly with an understanding that this is talking about the Holy Spirit or the human spirit, but there are some places where the translators have a problem. In the different translations of the New Testament there are many variations as to which is capitalized and which is small.

The New Translation by Darby and the New American Standard versions are very scholarly works, and one of the reasons why they are in such agreement down the line on interpretation is both the New American Standard committee and Darby, when he was translating, understood that man is body, soul, and spirit. In many circles, today, they do not understand this matter of man's trilogy. But even in II Corinthians 3, Darby and the New American Standard differ on the first spirit in verses 5b-6 which says, "Our adequacy is from God, who also made us adequate as servants of a new covenant, not of the letter, but of the Spirit." That word *Spirit* in my New American Standard is capitalized but if you have a Darby it is a small letter. Then it says, "For the letter kills, but the Spirit gives life." That is capitalized in both versions. I wonder why Darby changed. (Actually, there is a very good reason because it is an understanding. Darby is saying that what Paul was referring to is that the nature of the new covenant is of spirit by nature. The New American translators felt that when it is talking about the new covenant it is saying the source is the Spirit and not the letter. You can see there is a little problem here as to which one you choose.

The other one is in II Corinthians 11:4, "For if one comes and preaches another Jesus whom we have not preached, or you receive a different spirit..."Here, the New American Standard has made it small because to the New American committee, there is only one spirit that gets a capital and that is the Holy Spirit and if there is another spirit, you make it small. I do not know why Darby kept it with a capital, but he is a respected scholar and knows more than I do.

And if I could ask him, I would probably get a good answer.

The fact of the matter is that when the Holy Spirit comes into our spirit, there is a union there. What does it mean to pray in the Spirit, to speak in the Spirit? We have to understand there is a paradox involved here that makes it a little difficult to know which is which because if somebody prays in the Spirit, he is obviously praying in such a way that, transparently, God is speaking through him the will of God. Yet, God never pushes a man out of the way or have somebody pray like a robot, as if in some kind of trance, which is done all over the world in many religions today. But there is no trance among Christian people. He uses a human vessel that speaks His mind and there is a paradox there which is wonderful to behold. It is the same way with speaking in the Spirit that is a paradox. The Holy Spirit is veiled to some degree.

Veiled In The Fellowship Of The Saints

The third veiling that we find is the veil that He has in unity in the fellowship of the saints, in the corporate unity that He is involved. He is in fellowship with us. What is fellowship? This word *koinonia*, the communion of the Holy Spirit is the koinonia of the Holy Spirit. This Greek word *koinonia* means sharing all things in common. In the book of Acts we see the early church sharing their goods, sharing their food, sharing their homes, sharing their prayers, sharing their testimonies, sharing their burdens one with another, sharing all things in common. But at the deepest levels of fellowship, it is more than just the sharing of things, it is the sharing of the very life of Christ one with another. In I John 1, John said, "After being open to the fellowship with the Father and His Son, now I declare unto you the things of Christ that I have seen and touched and handled so that you can join this fellowship too." This is the most wonderful miracle, that through the fellowship of the Holy Spirit that John has received, He now fellowships with other saints life as he shares Jesus. Others come into this new life, entering into this fulness of joy as they join into this fellowship. This is a most amazing thing that we, as human beings, can actually share this life, this uncreated Zoe Life with one another. If the Holy Spirit has fellowshiped Christ in us, now we have something to give to somebody else.

We see here a most amazing mystery that the Holy Spirit is involved in but it is a unity hid within the fellowship of the saints. What do I mean? When we fellowship together, whether it is at a time of ministry like this, whether it is the fellowship time after the morning meeting, whether it is around the meal table, or whether it is in the prayer time early in the morning, if we have true fellowship, we fellowship the things of Christ. So we fellowship life one with another as we fellowship Christ through the fellowship of the Holy Spirit among the fellowship of the saints. Now we have a three-fold fellowship going on and the Holy Spirit is working there fellowshiping Christ with us so that as we fellowship with one another, it is a fellowship of life. The Holy Spirit is at work; He is involved. It may sound like a great mystery to you, and it is a great mystery how we can share life with one another, but it is a fact and a blessing in our communion with the Holy Spirit.

Now all of this veilness, all of this deferential nature, all of this hiddenness that we have been talking about might be a fact of the Holy Spirit's working in this dispensation, but it is no excuse for any Christian who has been born again, who loves the word of God, and who has been made a partaker of the Holy Spirit not to know who He is. We not only have the word of God, but we have the Holy Spirit who is clearly within the word of God and working in our lives but, sometimes, we do not know who He is. If we could really ask people who the Holy Spirit is, of course, first we would get some Trinitarian answer—Father, Son and Holy Spirit—stacked up, and there He is. But practically speaking, our problem is not theological; our problem is in our perspective regarding the Holy Spirit. I must say that many times the Holy Spirit is demeaned in His personhood by an ignorance as to who He really is, and if we want to have fellowship with the Holy Spirit, we must come to know who He really is—truly God, a Person, co-equal, co-existent with God. We need to come and know this Person.

MISCONCEPTIONS OF THE HOLY SPIRIT

An Impersonal Power

Many Christians, today, know that He is a Person in theory. Practically speaking though, He is an impersonal power that can be tapped into, used to serve God. "I want to work for God, so I find out some gift, some power I tap into and now I can serve God." You can go anywhere in the United States today and attend seminars that will teach you all of the gifts of the Holy Spirit. Then they will pray for you to receive any one you want and teach you how to use this gift in such a way that the Spirit will move in the meetings that you work. Think about that: the Spirit is just some impersonal force that can be used by Christians. I don't think so. He is a Person.

The Holy Spirit has a will. It says in I Corinthians 12:11, "The Spirit distributes severally to each one as He wills." You can pray and cut your arms and pray the prayers of Baal all day long for a spiritual gift but if it is not the Spirit's will, all you get is a counterfeit if you keep insisting. Behind this impersonal understanding there is also this notion that the gifts and the power of the Holy Spirit are the secret to ministry. I want to tell everybody that my conviction is in knowing the Enabler that enables somebody to minister, and He distributes the gifts as He designs.

The word gift, *charisma,* comes from the word *charis*—grace. Charisma is grace made tangible and the Holy Spirit can minister and use you in a situation if you will listen to *His* voice and know *His* leading and obey *Him.* But to say, "We do not want You, we want the presents" is like a kid who comes in for his birthday and starts ripping the presents open and does not care who they are from. "Don't show me the cards, just let me see the presents."

The Holy Spirit is not an *it.* When Peter responded to the people on the day of Pentecost, He said, "Repent and be baptized for the remission of sins and you will receive the gift of the Holy Spirit." Now there is a gift and He is the giver of whatever gifts come from that gift. He is not an impersonal power; He is a living Person and He gets grieved when He is treated as if He were some tool. He is not a tool and you do not use His tools without asking Him.

Nonessential For The Christian Life

The second common misconception regarding the Holy Spirit is that He is nonessential for the Christian life. He is essential if you want to be a minister. If you minister, you pray for an anointing but He only comes down on occasion. He is like a good angel. You notice how on TV and in movies now, everybody is obsessed with angels. The Holy Spirit makes a good angel. He shows up when things are down, when we need a miracle, something dreadful has happened, or we pray for a revival: "Please, Holy Spirit, show up. You have not been here for ten years but now we need You." Or He is like some kind of leprechaun—He shows up, He does something, He disappears. He is skittish and shy. You cannot get hold of Him. He just comes whenever He wants. He is undependable but He is very good.

The tragedy is, I lived among Christian people when I was first saved and they said, "Thank God, you are saved; now do the best you can in your own strength. Read the Bible, be faithful, don't you smoke, drink, dance or chew; just do it." You say, "Well, how?" "You just do it. You are born again, now you can do it." We never knew the daily indwelling, the listening, the obeying, the enabling, the comforting, the Helper. We did not even know there was such a thing. You may find that quite amazing but throughout the world there are many people who would say, as they said in Acts 19: "I do not even know who the Holy Spirit is"; and yet, they are Christians. But He is just some occasional phantom who shows up and helps. We are awfully glad when He comes but we do not know how to get Him here and we do not know where He goes to. So, we just live our lives by ourselves. Then you should live your life without breathing; let's start right now. That is how foolish that notion is! But there are some people who never pray and ask Jesus Christ to help them by the Holy Spirit to work on their jobs. They never pray, "Help me to raise my family," and expect this enabling to come from the indwelling presence of the Holy Spirit. How much we need this communion even of this One we say we do not know.

Taking His Presence For Granted

Of course, the most dangerous misconception is this: There are those who have become familiar with His presence and they take it for granted. They exploit His patience and His grace because they have learned that He will always be there. He will always comfort, take care, serve you, and help you. He will always lead you when you bother to ask. This is the most dangerous kind of misunderstanding. You just take advantage of Him. You have gotten used to Him so if He pokes your conscience, you do not listen anymore. If He would speak to you, you disobey. If He tries to discipline, you shun His discipline, yet, you know you can trade upon His faithful presence should you really get into trouble. He is your insurance policy for whatever you need; you are comfortable with the Holy Spirit.

Are we comfortable with the Holy Spirit? Then we do not know Him as we ought to know Him. If we misunderstand and abuse His loving patience and take advantage of Him, we are going to learn a lesson. He is God and He is Lord and He will not be trifled with. Oh, His patience is amazing but after a while, He will quit playing

30

around because He has a concentrated purpose to present us faultless before the Lord Jesus. He has a concentrated purpose to conform us to the image of Jesus Christ and He will not allow Himself to be abused. It is not even for His own sake but for the sake of Jesus Christ that He will not allow us to stay in this misunderstanding for long.

I was recently reading a book written by a very well known Bible teacher throughout the world. He was talking about many things, but one of the things he mentioned was that he never saw anywhere in the Bible and still is not convinced that there is anywhere in the Bible that it says we should pray to the Holy Spirit. The reason he gave was that the Holy Spirit is not our servant; He is God's servant. You do not go into a person's house and tell their servant what to do. If you need something done, you go to the master and ask the master if the servant could please do something. I thought that was very interesting and true, at least to this degree. Now don't get all choked up about this thing, but I am not so sure we should be praying to the Holy Spirit. He is sent by Jesus and the Father to do the will of God. We should rather surrender ourselves to His Lordship and ask what He wants. But if we have a need for something that we know from the Scriptures is fulfilled by the Holy Spirit, then let's ask the Lord Jesus who is the One who has given us the Holy Spirit for this ministry to be done. There is a proper respect of the Holy Spirit that needs to be recovered in the church if we are to fully live in this communion of the Holy Spirit. He is truly God and I want to declare Him as truly God in such a way that we might turn to Him and see who He is and ask the Lord to help us to enter into a real redemptive communion with the Holy Spirit. Otherwise, our communion with the Holy Spirit will only be occasional when it should be always. How can we live and fellowship with the Holy Spirit? We need to treat Him as He is—He is God.

THE HOLY SPIRIT AS GOD

I just want to mention six things about the Holy Spirit as God, as we think about Him as the Person that He is. This is only for the purpose of our meditation that we might understand that the Holy Spirit is God Himself.

The Holy Spirit Is Mighty God

He is mighty God. The Holy Spirit—mighty God. He is omniscient—all wise; He is omnipotent—all powerful; He is omnipresent—He is everywhere. David says, "Where can I flee from Thy Spirit?" He is omnipresent and He is all wise God. These are Latin words that were used by the early church, the patristic fathers who tried to define who the Spirit is. But the Bible has a much more profound picture of the Holy Spirit, the mighty God, when it says that the Spirit is the wind and the breath of God.

In Genesis 1:1-2 it says, "In the beginning God created the heavens and the earth. And the earth was formless and void, and darkness was over the surface of the deep; and the Spirit of God was moving over the surface of the waters." We see the Spirit, the wind of God brooding over the waters at creation and the implication in verse 2 is that there is a formlessness there that the Holy Spirit is about to set in order. The mighty God is about to set creation in order at the command of the word of God. So the word of God speaks: "Let there be celestial beings in the universe," and they are there in the twinkling of an eye. The mighty God orders the stars in their galaxies, places the planets in their solar systems, and sets the moons around the planets in the twinkling of an eye. It says in Psalm 33:6, "By the word of the Lord the heavens were made, and by the breath [or by the Spirit] of His mouth all their host." The mighty God, the Holy Spirit ordered these things in the universe.

Then the Lord God said, "Let there be plants," and 351,000 species of plants were set in their final order and places. He did not put coconut trees up in New York. By His might and power these things were created and placed in their order by the work of the word of God and the Holy Spirit working hand in hand. Who knows who did what? What was the big bang anyway? Was it the Lord when He spoke and it banged or was it the Holy Spirit with His hand when He went whoosh. Things were set in order because the Holy Spirit is mighty God, Creator God, along with the Father and the Son. You will never be able to untangle who did what in the creation of this world. The Holy Spirit had His wonderful hand in it.

In Psalm 104:29-30, it says that all of the animals were created by God the Spirit. God said, "Let there be the animals," and 853,000 species of animals (800,000 of them being insects, by the way), in a moment of time were created and set all over the universe. There again, the elephants were not put up in New York. There was an order, there was a power, there was a progress, there was a mighty work that the Holy Spirit and He alone could do. He ordered this thing. He knows how to order things. He is a God of order and a God of power.

Then it says that He is the very breath of life within each of these animals and when He removes His breath, the animals die and when He breathes again, the animals are born. He stooped down after God made up this clay ball that is called man and He breathed this breath of God, the Spirit of God into the nostrils of man and man became a living soul made in the image of God. Now he is body, soul, and spirit. All that breath, all that Spirit, all that wind, all that is the mighty God is not to be disrespected as some kind of impersonal power. He was there in the beginning, and He has been with God forever, ordering creation, beautiful creation, as the almighty God that He is.

How necessary is breath to you? That is how mighty our God is, every one of us breathing. Can you imagine the ancients in the pre-scientific world being fascinated by why they breathed? They did not know about oxygen and carbon dioxide. They only knew to breathe and when they ran, they panted: "Why am I doing this? And why is it, when that man died, he stopped breathing?" Think about it. This is a great mystery, but it was revealed that this is the Spirit of God in a man's life.

How necessary is the wind? I read the most fascinating, scientific journalistic book. This man was asked to write an article on the seven wonders of the scientific world. So he wrote this book, starting with the seventh and worked down to the first. Do you know what the first wonder of the scientific world to this non-believing, godless man was? He said the most amazing miracle and astounding wonder in this whole universe is the earth itself. He said it is a living biosphere; it is not just a thing. He says the water, the carbon dioxide, the wind, the seasons, the angle of the rotation, the plants, the animals and the balance of the thing is the most amazing ego-system, bio-system in the universe. Our existence is enabled by that wind, blowing, changing the seasons, bringing in rain and all of these things. It is all a picture of the dependency in that transcendent way. Don't forget everyone in the Godhead—Father, Son and Holy Spirit—is both transcendent and eminent. He is over us, above us, and beyond us—that is transcendent. He is within us, He is working, He is present— that is eminent. The Holy Spirit is the wind, that which is working over and above us, working across the world, even blowing nations and blowing history for God's purpose as well as the breath within us, working that close, that eminent with us. This Holy Spirit is mighty God, mighty God.

The Holy Spirit Is Holy

The Holy Spirit is holy; He is fearful in holiness. The Holy Spirit, the living God, is fearful in holiness. Now I have an interesting Bible fact: Ninety-three times in the Bible the Spirit is called the Holy Spirit. How many times is Holy Spirit mentioned in the Old Testament? Three times; ninety times in the New Testament, but only three in the Old Testament. In Psalm 51:11 David says, "Take not Thy Holy Spirit from me." The other two are in Isaiah 63:10, 11 where it says, "But they rebelled and grieved His Holy Spirit ...; where is He who put His Holy Spirit in the midst of them." Only three times in the whole Old Testament is the Holy Spirit mentioned..

There is a fact of history that we should know. By the time Jesus came to this earth and by the time of the writing of the New Testament, the Jews called the Spirit the Holy Spirit. But in the Old Testament days they called Him the Spirit, the breath of God, the breath that fell upon Samson and enabled him to do miraculous things. By the New Testament time, He was called the Holy Spirit. Why is that? It is because they learned through the discipline of history, through the discipline of their idolatry, through the discipline of their captivity, through the discipline of their disobedience, that the Spirit is not to be trifled with. He is fearful, He is holy, He has a personality, He has a character. He is God, the fearful, holy God. That means He hates sin and He will mortify the deeds of the flesh, and it means He will change the atmosphere of any meeting or any family household where unChristlike things are done. As He grieves, He will change the atmosphere of the place until things are put right because He is a holy God. He is to be feared and those who do not fear Him are fools, the Bible says. Those who fear Him will become wise.

The Bible says that there were those who lied to the Holy Spirit and they lost their life. We find this in Acts 5:3. Peter said, "Ananias, why has Satan filled your heart to lie to the Holy Spirit?" Then at the end of verse 4 he says, "Why is it that you have conceived this deed in your heart? You have not lied to men, but to God." I just want you to see that the Holy Spirit is God, truly God, and Peter used this term interchangeably, even at the beginning of his understanding as a Christian.

The Holy Spirit is God, not the power of God; He is God. He is holy and He is to be feared. Those who lie to the Holy Spirit find their breath taken away. There were those who resisted the Holy Spirit when Stephen preached to the stiff-necked Israelites in Jerusalem about the fact, historically, that they had been stiff-necked and were always resisting the Spirit of God. It is possible, even though the Spirit is called in Hebrews 10 the Spirit of grace, to insult Him. How do we insult Him? Trample underfoot the Son of God or use the blood of Jesus Christ in an unworthy way or count it as an unholy thing and you have insulted the Spirit of grace. That passage in Hebrews 10, as you know, is one of the most frightening passages regarding severe discipline that is in the Bible.

Then, of course, God forbid that any should blaspheme the Holy Spirit. He is a fearful God and He is not to be trifled with because He is holy and we must realize that and give Him His due respect.

The Holy Spirit Is The Master Builder

He is the all wise master builder. What an engineer this Holy Spirit is! He is the hands of the potter. We have that wonderful picture in the Old Testament prophecy of the potter, our Father, shaping and molding us, and it is the Holy Spirit who is His hands. Think of His mighty power. Do you know what He is doing right now? I know we cannot conceive of this but I am going to say something right now which will just go in one ear and out the other because it is too much for us to take in. Right now He has in His hands the vessels of millions of Christians and He is molding them all singly into the one predestined image of Jesus Christ. What a master designer and craftsman, what a powerful shaper He is! At the same time, He is molding these millions of vessels all over this world right now, He is also planning and leading us through millions of circumstances, working them all together for good toward the one purpose of God. Think about that! He is arranging things, leading us here and there through circumstances simultaneously, at the same time. I do not know how He does it. How many hands does He have?

At the same time, He is coordinating our encounters and meetings with other vessels in such a way that we grow, we are edified, we are dealt with, we are knit together and made one. He so arranges that you listen to just the right radio preacher or read the right devotional book or read the Scripture that you needed for that day. He is arranging all of that stuff. He is a mighty and all wise God. Think of the dimension of this thing when you cast it across the world. He is a mighty God, the all wise master builder.

He is balancing things in our life. He takes discipline and balances it with encouragement so that you do not have too much that you have to bear. He knows how much you can deal with, and He also encourages and encourages. He arranges times of fellowship and blessing for you and also arranges times of necessary loneliness for you. He is leading you and getting you to respond to the good works that the Father has prepared beforehand that you should walk in. Then He enables you to do these good works and to bear fruit for God, and at the same time, He hinders you from doing works that are dead, works of the flesh, or works that are out of season. What an amazing balance here. Right now He is arranging and sensitizing vessels of supply to know about vessels of need so that the supply can meet need. Then He makes sure that things are reversed so that in some way the vessels of need will be vessels of supply and meet the vessels of need in such a way that there is an equality in the body of Christ. Everybody, in the end, will feel both indebted and useful. He is an amazing God. He is revealing to us the things of Jesus Christ, things which eyes have never seen nor ears heard, never have they entered into the heart of man. He is revealing all that we can possibly bear and He is withholding from us some things that we are not ready for. He is an incredible God. He is strengthening us with power through His Spirit in the inner man, building, building, building, strengthening us within so that Christ can dwell in our hearts through faith. At the very same time, He is absolutely bringing us to the end of ourselves, frustrating us, dealing with our old man, dealing with all our old reliances, our old habit patterns, our old wrong thinking, bringing us to death, and at the same time, strengthening us inside. This is a masterful job He is doing when you multiply that by the millions. He is a mighty God. He is the all wise master builder.

The Holy Spirit Is Completing All Things

He is the Holy Spirit that God sent out to gather in and to bring this age to its close. The Holy Spirit is the mighty wind that is blowing over history, that is blowing over nations, that is blowing over governments. Right now He holds world rulers in His hands. Over here He is hardening their hearts by provoking them according to God's counsel, and over here He is stirring the spirits of some world rulers to do things that they do not even understand why they are doing them, but it is for God's purpose, for God's goals, and God's glory that these things are being done.

I was amazed when I went to Nepal a few years ago and visited a few days. I saw a tremendous outpouring of the Holy Spirit with people being saved and the gospel going forth. It is an amazing story in Nepal right now, but the thing that I just could not believe was that I heard from the people in Nepal that Christianity had been illegal up to about 1990 when this monarchy was deposed and Christianity was allowed by the Communist government. Oh, the Holy Spirit is holding world rulers in His hands, opening doors that people might hear the gospel and then working over here in such a way as to purify the church. He knows what He is doing. It is way over our heads, but He has been sent out to bring this age to a conclusion. He is driving Israel to a desperate time and to their knees to truly seek the true and living God. They have tried everything on their own, tried everything by their wits, tried everything by their power, and they are being driven to their knees to seek the true and living God once again. You do realize that most of the people in Israel do not pray, many do not believe in God, but God is driving them to the place where they will look to the living God, even to the place where they pray and see the One whom they have pierced. The Lord is doing all these things.

He is confusing and overruling coalitions of power, evil men, terrorists, people who are bitter and trying to produce anarchy all across the world. But the Holy Spirit is the great restraining force over the whole earth, holding back the proliferation of evil until such time as He is drawn out of the way and the lawless one comes, and the end comes. The Holy Spirit, the great One, is sent out to do all these things.

He is even working in Christendom, frustrating the plans of those who are trying to build the tower of Babel. He takes their plans and breaks them down and causes a schism or does something in order to prevent man from building idols in the name of Christ. But at the same time, if He is to bring things to the end, He has been sent out according to the divine decree of God who said, "I will have Myself a remnant." If the Lord had not kept for Himself a remnant, the church would be as Sodom and Gomorrah. But it was declared in heaven: "I will have Myself a remnant of people who call upon My name from a pure heart who have not bowed their knees to Baal," and the Spirit is being sent out across this world. This work is being done not by might of preaching, not by power organizations, but by the Spirit, says the Lord. He goes to the deadest places, valleys of dry bones, where the Christians are discouraged, hopeless, and heartless, and they have given up. He breathes on them and the living hope comes into them. A vision comes to them and they find grace to stand up and begin to overcome and take up the cross of the Lord Jesus and bear faithful testimony to Him. This is being done all over the world. The Lord is setting Himself up a witness standard in every nation of the world and then He will come back. But right now the Spirit is being sent out into the highways and the hedges to bring back and compel all who call upon the name of Jesus, back to the Father's house that His house might be full.

The Holy Spirit Is The Promise Of The Father

He is the God of promise to every seeking heart. He is promised. Those awaiting the consolation of Israel understood what the promise was; it was a familiar phrase to a good Jew. What is the promise? All those who were waiting for Jesus to come, those who were waiting around the temple, as we read in the story of Luke, were awaiting the consolation of Israel. They were waiting for the promise. What is the promise? The promise is that the Messiah will come and He will pour out His Spirit on this world again. All were waiting for a living word. But even those in the Old Testament were waiting for the Spirit to be poured out again, to hear a living word and for God to do it. They were waiting for the promise of the Father. That is what the Spirit was called among those awaiting the consolation.

He was the Spirit promised to the Gentiles as well: "In the last days I will pour out My Spirit upon all flesh." During this period of time of this outpoured, promised Spirit, whosoever calls on the name of the Lord will be saved irrespective of person. Whether they are maidservants or whether they are the head of the household, whoever calls on the name of the Lord will be saved and the Spirit will pour life out upon them. He is the promised Holy Spirit to all who call out with a seeking heart.

He is the promised Comforter. Jesus said, "I am going away but to the church I will send a Comforter." He is promised and He comes just as He promised. He brings us new birth, He renews our mind, He clothes us in righteousness, He empowers us with an endowment from on high.

Then He purifies us, He sanctifies us, He illumines the word of God to us, and He reveals Jesus to us. He works day and night in our lives because He is the promised Comforter who has come. What a wonderful God! He transforms us, He perfects us, and He employs us in bidding others come and receive of the life.

Right now, the Holy Spirit has gone out across the world even while we are speaking here. It is the most amazing thing to conceive how the Holy Spirit is in so many places at once, but after all, He is omnipresent. He is meeting the needs of every seeking heart. Somewhere, there is a martyr who has been faithful for the Lord. He has lost everything, He is all alone, He is in jail, but the Spirit is there. Somebody is mourning and the Spirit is there, comforting them. There is somebody who is ready to depart in peace, a faithful soldier who, like Paul, has run his course in the race and the Spirit is preparing his soul, getting him ready. He is looking homeward already. He remembers the orphans whom nobody loves, even way across the world when we see the pitiful pictures of the children whose parents have been killed in some conflict in Africa or elsewhere. But for every seeking heart, the Holy Spirit exercises the true religion of remembering them, of helping them. There are widows, precious sisters who have lost their husbands, and no one cares or loves them, but the Holy Spirit has been sent out as the promised Comforter.

There are some people right now who, because they love the Lord, are banded together and are praying because the world has placed them in a predicament they cannot possibly get out of and they wonder: "How are we going to live in this place with this government and with this evil?" They do not know what to do but they are seeking God and He has given them a word of wisdom on how to escape, how to live in that place. He has given them a way to refute the wisdom of the world and to live even in the midst of impossible situations. The Holy Spirit has been sent out as the promised One to every seeking heart.

He is all wise and maybe even down the way, He is compelling, with His conviction, prodigal teenagers who are living in the world's pigsties and He has convicted them: "That is not the place to be." He is telling them about the Father's house and the grace of the Lord Jesus and the communion of the Holy Spirit, compelling them to turn around and go back home to their house and to their Father and to their salvation. I thank God for that.

I remember when some of you were teenagers in the teenage group and I just about gave up on you. But here you are in the Father's house. It is amazing! No matter how messed up a teenager gets, as soon as he turns his heart, there is the Holy Spirit leading him right down the road back home.

The Holy Spirit Is The Loving Servant Of God

He is God, the loving Servant, diligent, focused in His love upon the Son of God. He is the loving Servant of God. He has the best attitude you have ever seen in a servant. He is ecstatic, He is buoyant about His service, unlike any service we have ever seen, because He is focused upon the Father and upon the Son. He is God the Servant, God the loving Servant. He has set His face, and His will is determined that He is going to reveal Christ and glorify Christ in everything He does until the knowledge of the glory of the Lord fills the earth. He is a loving servant.

He is searching every corner of the depth of God. He is searching every corner of the height, of the width, of the depth, and the breadth of the love of Christ to reveal unto us when we gather together. Isn't that amazing? We come together and He shows us and we begin to comprehend just how wide and how high. It is the Holy Spirit searching the depth of God to bring us this information. He is the loving Servant, bent on His purpose, willing to do. He is the faithful scribe writing on every heart. What does He write— doctrine, knowledge, how to escape? On every heart He is writing, "Jesus Christ, Jesus Christ," with indelible Holy Spirit ink. He is the faithful Scribe.

The Holy Spirit Is A Faithful Intercessor

He is a faithful Intercessor. He is groaning for us, and we do not even understand. We want the will of God, but we do not even know how to say it, so we feel the groan inside. Isn't it an amazing thing? You just sense it. We gather together, we sense our fellowship life, we are happy to be together but we sense some groaning. He is working in our lives; He is making us dissatisfied. You know, I am not satisfied with where I am, nor where our fellowship is. I cannot be satisfied because He has a groan in me and until this whole thing is worked out His way, I will not be satisfied. He has placed that groan in here and He is the One groaning even when I quit the groaning. He is a faithful intercessor.

The Holy Spirit Is A Ready Teacher

He is a ready Teacher. Do you know how ready He must be? If we just think of it now, as staggering as it may be, all over this world He is breathing upon the word of God with everybody who has opened their Bible. Every saint who has come and asked, "Holy Spirit of God, show me Jesus, show me Your will as I open the word of God." There are 2,133 languages, according to the Wyecliff translators, and He can breathe upon each one of them and bring Jesus to people. The Holy Spirit is some kind of faithful Teacher.

The Holy Spirit Is a Persistent Counselor

He is a persistent Counselor. He is always convincing us just like with the disciples. They had to be convinced by many infallible proofs that Jesus was alive. Even though they knew He was alive, yet they had to be proven again and again over forty days. Many times they had to be convinced and convinced again. Now the Holy Spirit is that Counselor. He will not leave us alone. He brings us into court and says, "No, Jesus is alive." Our doubting hearts are convinced by the Holy Spirit. He says, "You do not believe, I will show you again. You do not believe, I will show you again," until we are convinced that Jesus is alive. Oh, may we not just say the words, but may we sense the reality that Jesus is alive.

This Counselor has been sent to win the argument, to convince us that Jesus is alive and that He is Lord of all, not just some man but Lord of all, Lord of the universe, and Lord of all things. Then, this Counselor convinces us and He places the secret into our heart whereby we know that Jesus is all. Even though He strips away from us things we thought were important, He places the

54

secret into our hearts and we know that Jesus is all.

Sometimes, I think Christians are schizophrenics because when you see a brother or a sister doing something like giving an announcement, looking like a human being and then, in just an instant, at the thought of Jesus, some tears rush to their eyes. You say, "My, how that person loves Jesus but how well he conceals it most of the time." We have a secret but, in some sense, we are ashamed to tell the secret all the time because it seems so unnatural to us. But even as we walk on this earth as normal human beings, we have a secret in our hearts and it is this, "I know Jesus loves me and I love Him so much, but I am embarrassed to say it too much because I do not think people believe me because I clown around so much. They would not understand that I have a secret: Jesus is everything; I cannot live without Him. But I am ashamed to tell the secret because of living in this world." The Holy Spirit has convinced us it is no longer a secret, to let it out and show people that Jesus is your all.

He is a loving Servant. He is a servant of love. He is absolutely determined that He is going to pour out the love of God into our hearts and keep pouring out the love of God into our hearts until we get so full that we have to pass Him along. Shed abroad into our hearts by the Holy Spirit, this faithful Servant of God is ministering the love of the Father and the love of the Son to us all the time.

Of course, He is always the Servant of the cross. In His duty and in His delight He is jealously guarding the house of God. He will not allow anything of our flesh, anything of our natural man, anything that is of the enemy to get into the house of God. He guards at the door and brings us to the cross and to the end of ourselves; then He lets resurrection life through. He is a Servant of the cross and He stands for that purpose until the church is glorious and without spot and wrinkle. He is the Spirit of God.

We have talked about this Spirit of God, this mighty God, this servant of God, this God sent out, this holy, awesome God, but do we know this Holy Spirit? The time is too short to just fool around about the Holy Spirit. If we want to commune with the Holy Spirit we are going to have to enter into a relationship with the Holy Spirit who is holy, mighty God. We need to repent more than we need knowledge. We have treated Him with despite, we have allowed Him to live in our midst as an acquaintance, and He is not satisfied. We should repent of that. We are not going to gain any more knowledge if we are just trying to gain knowledge with our natural mind. But if we are willing to repent of grieving the Holy Spirit in some way, of quenching the Holy Spirit, of being prejudiced against the Holy Spirit, of blocking the progress of the Holy Spirit, then He will fill us with the love of Christ. We should not quench the Holy Spirit, nor insult the Holy Spirit, nor resist the Holy Spirit, but we should, today, if we hear His voice, harden not our hearts.

This wonderful provision we have, the grace of our Lord Jesus Christ, the love of God and the fellowship of the Holy Spirit, is ours to live and to abide in. It is a precious treasure; it is the best God can give. He is giving Himself, Father, Son and Holy Spirit, but we must understand who He is aright or we will not live in the good of it. He is a Person; He is God. He wants to be part of our lives, hands on, intimate basis, talking and communing, but He is a living Person. We need to get rightly related to Him.

We need to realize who He is. It seems a strange thing to say that the Holy Spirit needs to reveal to us who He is but we need such revelation. We need to understand this. It would make a lot of difference in our lives if we really knew who He is. He wants to commune with us but there is a change, a shift of relationship as to just exactly who is the boss in this relationship and we need to get honest with Him.

Let's pray:

We thank You, Father, for the precious Scriptures that speak of Your Spirit everywhere and speak of His love for us, His desire to serve all the purpose of the Father and all the desires of the Son. We thank You for the precious Holy Spirit. Lord, in our hearts we can only think of what disservice we have given, blind as the Corinthians to the fact that the Holy Ghost dwells among us. How easily we found our ability to just be in the natural man, how easy to disobey, how easily we ignore His prompting, His leading, and quell the conscience that stirred.

Oh God, living God, mighty God, we love You as You are. We sense Your entreating desire upon our lives. We have listed in some short measure some of the benefits of this life. Oh, that we could enter in. We forsake all ignorance, all thought of our being able to live without You, all thought of Your being some impersonal, uninvolved power. We bow before a mighty God, a Person with whom we have to do.

Oh Lord, we come and embrace the fulness of our salvation and the fulness of our inheritance. We take hold of this precious inheritance and down payment that we have been given from heaven and take Him as our possession and thank You that He owns us. Oh Lord Jesus, enthroned Master, pour out the Person upon our lives in such a way as to effect a change individually and corporately. Oh, let it be that we might be by the enabling of Your anointing to become sensitized to who You are and to embrace the fulness of Your love. We want to live in the good of our salvation.

We know we talk so much. Oh, we want You to lead us. You are the great inspiring conductor of our worship. You are the One who writes the songs and leads us to worship our Lord Jesus and conducts us in our worship.

Oh Lord, we come and thank You, Father, Son and Holy Spirit, living God. We cannot quite separate You in all of the pieces but we want to embrace our God given to us through Jesus Christ. We know the Holy Spirit is a Person but we know He will not move at our command. We know He comes in the name of Jesus. He comes as we look to Your face. We dare not glance over and try to look at the Holy Spirit but just cast our eyes upon Jesus and find the Holy Spirit near and dear. Lord Jesus, work upon us, baptize us in the Holy Spirit, make us very aware of His precious presence. That alone that will bring us to the perfection that you desire in our lives

Oh, precious Spirit of God, what a friend, what a help! We feel you in the background. We wish to know You more but we look away to our Lord, knowing that this is the way to know You more. We thank You, we love You. In Jesus' name. Amen.

THE MINISTRY OF THE HOLY SPIRIT

Luke 24:49—And behold, I am sending forth the promise of My Father upon you; but you are to stay in the city until you are clothed with power from on high.

Acts 1:4-5—And gathering them together, He commanded them not to leave Jerusalem, but to wait for what the Father had promised, "Which," He said, "you heard of from Me; for John baptized with water, but you shall be baptized with the Holy Spirit not many days from now."

Acts 2:1-4—And when the day of Pentecost had come, they were all together in one place. And suddenly there came from heaven a noise like a violent, rushing wind, and it filled the whole house where they were sitting. And there appeared to them tongues as of fire distributing themselves, and they rested on each one of them. And they were all filled with the Holy Spirit and began to speak with other tongues, as the Spirit was giving them utterance.

Acts 2:14-21—But Peter, taking his stand with the eleven, raised his voice and declared to them: "Men of Judea, and all you who live in Jerusalem, let this be known to you, and give heed to my words. For these men are not drunk, as you suppose, for it is only the third hour of the day; but this is what was spoken of through the prophet Joel: 'And it shall be in the last days,' God says, 'That I will pour forth of My Spirit upon all [flesh] mankind; and your sons and your daughters shall prophesy, and your young men shall see visions, and your old men shall dream dreams; even upon My bondslaves, both men and women, I will in those days pour forth of My Spirit and they shall prophesy. And I will grant wonders in the sky above, and signs on the earth beneath, blood, and fire, and vapor of smoke. The sun shall be turned into darkness and the moon into blood, before the great and glorious day of the Lord shall come. And it shall be, that everyone who calls on the name of the Lord shall be saved.'

Acts 2:32-33—This Jesus God raised up again, to which we are all witnesses. Therefore having been exalted to the right hand of God, and having received from the Father the promise of the Holy

Spirit, He has poured forth this which you both see and hear.

John 15:26-27—When the Helper [the Holy Spirit] comes, whom I will send to you from the Father, that is the Spirit of truth, who proceeds from the Father, He will bear witness of Me, and you will bear witness also, because you have been with Me from the beginning.

John 16:7-8—But I tell you the truth, it is to your advantage that I go away; for if I do not go away, the Helper shall not come to you; but if I go, I will send Him to you. And He, when He comes, will convict the world concerning sin, and righteousness, and judgment; concerning sin, because they do not believe in Me; and concerning righteousness, because I go to the Father and you no longer behold Me; and concerning judgment, because the ruler of this world has been judged. I have many more things to say to you, but you cannot bear them now. But when He, the Spirit of truth, comes, He will guide you into all the truth; for He will not speak on His own initiative, but whatever He hears, He will speak; and He will disclose to you what is to come. He shall glorify

Me; for He shall take of Mine, and shall disclose it to you. All things that the Father has are Mine; therefore I said, that He takes of Mine, and will disclose it to you.

In these Scriptures, which tell us some of the ministry of the Holy Spirit, we find ourselves involved with the triune God—Father, Son, and Holy Spirit. The Holy Spirit comes to commune with us and what He communes and fellowships and shares with us are the things regarding Jesus and the things which belong to Jesus, because the Father gave them to Him. Jesus and the Father own the same things, so He shares the things of the Father with us and the Father shares the things of the Son with us. It is the Holy Spirit who brings us this blessed fellowship. We are the recipients of this most blessed benediction. We receive the grace of our Lord Jesus Christ, we experience the love of God shed abroad in our hearts, and we sense, always, the Holy Spirit working, speaking, and sharing the things of Christ.

As part of our salvation we are given communion with the Holy Spirit. But how do we react to this communion? Some Christians are afraid of the Holy Spirit. Teenagers are often afraid of the fellowship of the Holy Spirit because they are sure that if they talk to Him, He will convict them—and He will! But the communion of the Holy Spirit is blessed and if we see Him as the Person He is, a loving God, all-mighty, all-wise, a wonderful God, we will want to have fellowship with Him. He is our hope in every conceivable way.

THE MINISTRY OF THE HOLY SPIRIT AS WIND AND BREATH

I want to share more on the communion of the Holy Spirit by looking at His ministry. Although the New Testament is filled with many matters of His ministry, I want to break down the comprehensive ministry of the Holy Spirit in a simple, two-fold way. I want us to look at the Holy Spirit as both the *wind* and the *breath*. You remember that both the Hebrew and Greek words for "spirit" can also mean either breath or wind. He is the divine Wind, that power that we see always on the move, moving things, people, even governments, especially in the gospel of

Luke and the book of Acts. But He is also the divine Breath, the very intimate life of the Holy Spirit, that which we read about in the gospel of John, I John and in Paul's letters. There is both the wind and the breath. He is the wind that is sent out on a mission into the world to convict the world of sin and righteousness and judgment. We read in Luke 24:49 that He has been sent forth from God. The Greek word for *He has been sent forth* is "Apostello," the verb form of the word "apostolos." He is now the divine apostle sent out to bear witness. This is His present mission over the whole world, a convicting, saving mission.

He is also the breath; He has the ministry of life inside the believer. Besides the broadcasting without, He is speaking within. There is this ministry of life not only inside every believer but among believers. As the wind, we see His ministry upon the church. In the book of Acts, we see groups of apostles and prophets and evangelists moving as the Wind blew them from place to place, preaching the gospel, establishing churches. But in order to have fulness, we see that in every place established by the wind of the

Spirit, there is also ministry of the Breath within the body of Christ as she is built up in love from the inward supply of every member. This is the ministry of the Holy Spirit. It is not just the wind ministering upon the church but the life within the church itself—the wind and the breath.

The Wind of the Spirit

We see that the wind is powerful and the wind is initial, blowing things into creation, blowing churches into being; but we also see the breath. The breath is the life, the breath is the continuity. It is the breath that brings things to perfection. The breath is there all the time, every day breathing, breathing. The wind moves in mighty ways, performing miraculous things, but the fulness of the ministry of the Spirit involves an understanding that there is a relationship between these two, and wherever this relationship is present and evident, God can do what He wants to do. We can see so clearly in the book of Acts the church under this influence of the Holy Spirit, being moved by the wind, being enlivened and built up by the breath. We see in Acts the rushing wind moving the saints out with the gospel, bringing conviction to people with the preaching of the gospel, performing great signs as the witness moves out in four different areas starting from Jerusalem, out to Judea, then to Samaria, then to the uttermost parts of the earth. Who can say how this wind will move? In a sovereign way He knows just where to go, just where to blow, just what city to hit. You see this in the book of Acts, and it is a wonderful, exciting story.

In Acts 5:32 we find one of many statements that shows the Christians co-working together with the Holy Spirit in a joint bearing of witness of the resurrection of Jesus Christ, and as they go this wind is blowing. Peter stands up and says, "We are witnesses of these things; and so is the Holy Spirit, whom God has given to those who obey Him."

The Breath of the Spirit

The wind was blowing in the book of Acts but the breath was blowing as well. They not only preached the gospel, they lived the life of Jesus Christ. In Acts 2:42, they continued steadfastly in the apostles' doctrine and fellowship, in breaking of bread and of prayers. You see that the church not only ministered; the church lived. They shared things together; they waited on the Lord in prayer; they offered worship to Him; they communed; they remembered the Lord's great love for them together. They knew this breath breathing daily on the church. They went down to the temple, to Solomon's porch, and heard the apostles tell the stories of Jesus and saw them sometimes perform great miracles within the presence of a crowd. But also from house to house, day to day, they experienced the fellowship of the Spirit together and the Lord added daily to the church those who were being saved. It was the wind; it was the breath. It is one Spirit. We are not talking about some schizophrenic power, but a two-fold operation as the Spirit is allowed to minister in fulness upon the church and upon the world.

In Acts 4, when Peter and John were thrown into prison, the church went to prayer. They sought the Lord, and the Lord spoke to them with His breath. They took their stand upon Psalm 2, that the Lord reigns over those persecutors. They said, "Take note of their threats and grant us boldness to continue to preach the gospel. Just as they got through praying, the wind filled the sails again, gave them great boldness to preach, and many more were saved; but they were listening to the voice of the Lord.

In Acts 5, a matter of discipline came up in the church where Ananias and Sapphira were lying to the Holy Spirit. Everyone saw firsthand that you just do not go blowing around and ministering. You have to be true to the testimony. They learned by the breath of the Spirit this serious matter of discipline in walking in the light.

In Acts 6, we see that the church was growing, but with growing pain there were some needs. There were some people not being fed and treated properly. So the brothers went to praying, and rather than trying to do it all themselves, they felt the Lord saying that this was an opportunity to share responsibility. They were to find some suitable men and pray for them, which they did. The next thing you know it says "and the word increased among them." As a result of them listening to the breath of the Lord when a problem came up in the church life, the wind was able to continue to blow freely and fruitfully over the land.

In Acts 8 we find an example of the relationship and the perfect unity of wind and breath in the ministry of Philip. First, he was preaching to a multitude in the city of Samaria. The wind was blowing and many came to the Lord, seeing the wonders and signs that he was doing as he proclaimed the resurrection of Jesus as Lord and Christ. But in the midst of this time he heard the breath: "Go to the desert." He does not say, "I cannot go to the desert; my ministry is too important here in the city." He left this revival, as we would call it, to go in obedience to the voice of the Spirit out into the desert where he found that Ethiopian man who opened the door to the church in Africa. Oh, it is so important not only to know the wind but to know the breath.

When Saul was converted in Acts 9, it says that after he had taken food and was strengthened, he began testifying of Jesus Christ from his knowledge of Scripture. The next thing you know, after being let down in a basket, he showed up in Jerusalem and started preaching the gospel. Do you know what the saints did? They heard him preaching, they saw the controversies he was stirring up, and the apostles said, "Paul, here is a ticket back to Tarsus. You need some work inside. You need to go back home. There is some breathing you need among the brethren." They did not doubt his ministry, his anointing, the power of the Spirit upon him, his knowledge. They saw something in this man, but they could say to him, "Hold it, hold it, not so fast, young man. There is time for a little teaching by the breath of God. Go back home. There are some lessons for you to learn." And Paul went back in obedience to Tarsus.

In Acts 13, where the apostles were sent out from Antioch, we find them praying, fasting, worshiping. They did not just decide to go out: "Let's go out. We will throw a dart on a map and then go, and Jesus will be with us." No, they served faithfully and ministered at Antioch until the day the Holy Spirit said, "Set apart Saul and Barnabas." How did that happen? Was it a prophecy? Did Manaen or one of the brothers stand up and say, "Thus saith the Lord: the Lord says send out Saul and Barnabas." Maybe. That is the windy kind of way. But what if a brother just said, "You know, as we were praying, I just felt an impression, as if the breath said, 'I think it is time for Saul and Barnabas to go visit Barnabas' home town and minister.'" That is where they started out—in Cyprus. Then maybe others said, "You know, we've had the feeling that it is right that we send them out to other places as well." We will never know whether it was wind or breath because it makes no difference. We can say, "The Holy Spirit said." They moved according to that.

There was another instance in Acts 15 when a controversy arose that caused them to gather together. They were not so busy with the wind that they did not have time for life, for fellowship. Men brought forth very vehement arguments about why the Gentiles should be circumcised and one side said, "No, no, no," and the other side said, "Yes, yes, yes." All of this went on for a while as they fellowshiped together. It was quite a lively thing. We would call it an argument, but for the Jews it was just recreation. Then James, the one whom you would think would be least likely to stand with Paul and Barnabas and their mission, stood up and God gave him a word of wisdom, a spiritual gift, as it is called. He said, "I think we should not put anything else upon these Gentiles other than that they not eat meat sacrificed to idols, and so forth." As soon as James said this, it sounded good to the Holy Spirit, and a letter was sent out from the whole church. As a result the Gentile work, which could have been curtailed at that very moment, continued to expand and the wind kept blowing. We see such a beautiful unity there.

WHEN THE WIND AND BREATH ARE SEPARATED

When we see this unity in the book of Acts, we have to place this picture against the problems that we see today in the church. The wind gets separated from the breath, and when that happens, there is a guarantee that problems will arise. So today, for different reasons, Christians seem divided between the deeper life people (breath), and the Charismatics (wind). Historically, this dividing problem usually occurs something like this. The wind blows sovereignly where He wills and a new movement is started. Is it John Wesley? Is it Martin Luther? There is a blowing of the wind and the gospel is being preached. There is a community being born, there are signs and wonders and power and release. The wind is definitely blowing. It was blown by the will of God. But as this ministry commences, the breath begins to rise up and say, "Wait a minute, wait a minute, something is wrong." But they do not listen. The problem has usually been that men in ministry who are working in the wind ministry do not take time to stop and listen to the life of the Holy Spirit when something gets violated. They continue on faithful to the 'ministry' but no longer faithful to the Lord. Have you ever noticed how often our Lord Jesus was ministering in such and such a town and the Father pulled Him aside for a while for prayer and for seeking? But among God's servants, once a ministry has gained its own momentum, no one is willing to stop and problems are rolled over and inner issues of life are ignored. The next thing you know, you find a ministry with great power but there is no inner life to back it up. So the wind of the Spirit ceases but man continues on with his own kind of wind—a soul-driven wind—and windbags keep on preaching. But the Lord is no longer in the wind, and the more they preach, the less there is of the Spirit; the harder they work, the less fruit there is. But many are engaged in the work and there is the need of maintaining the ministry. Meanwhile, body life suffers. Where is the body ministry among the saints? Maybe the problem was that these workers were blowing with the wind, and the Spirit was blowing them somewhere else but they stayed. Do you know what happens when men with ministries stay in a place too long? They overwhelm the saints. The next thing you know, the church's ministry becomes just a few workers speaking to a large, passive audience but where is the body life? Where is the increase? Where is the life and the dealing and the coordination and submission one with another? All of this kind of loses its way. We have ministry and ministry and ministry, but the body becomes weak and the reality of the testimony is not there. There is a wind blowing but it is not the Holy Spirit anymore. The saints have become shallow, and they are doomed to a life of immaturity and carnality. They have to be kept in place by human authority. Somewhere the breath was missed. This has usually been our problem. When the big ball of ministry is rolling who will listen for the still, small breath?

By reading 1 Corinthians we can look into the life of the church in Corinth at just such a crucial stage in the ministry of the Spirit. They loved the wind but the breath began speaking to them of the cross. Will they listen?

They loved apostles. They say, "Please, send us more apostles, we love the ministry of apostles. We love the wind they bring. We love gifting. Show us how to do this, show us how to prophesy, we will practice. Come on, be with us. We love the wind; we love windy times." Paul says, "Do you know what you have done in your desire for power? You have begun to compete with one another. You have meetings where one guy is prophesying and another guy stands up, and they are competing as to who is better. Then there is a division in the church between those who like this apostle and those who like that apostle. And then you have a dispute over the order of importance of this gift and those who just have a little one. You have those with a weak conscience and those with knowledge and all kinds of things because of carnality." But thank God, through the faithfulness of Paul, the breath of the Spirit was saying, "You need the cross. This is human wisdom, and it will not float." If the church of Corinth listens, then the wind comes back in line with the breath and there is fulness. It is the way of God. The breath should control the wind. This is the restraint of God that keeps any move of God in life. But every move of God that starts out by windy grace will come to the crossroads where the Lord will apply the cross and say, "Turn aside, pray, seek My face and deal with this reality." Unless they heed that, after a while, their own wind will blow them way off the track.

Some great movements of God are not even existent anymore because they stopped listening when the anointing warned of violation, when the inner breath of the Spirit was trying to talk. In God's mercy, He waits a while and then blows again somewhere else. He begins to blow and to move people and they begin to see something. They begin to be faithful to Him and He begins to honor them. This gracious move begins again, but unless the saints can develop the character of Christ, they cannot handle the wind. Unless the saints are built in the life of the Holy Spirit's communion, after a while, the wind becomes void.

This pattern of life is just like the history in the book of Judges. Those people had no character. God kept raising up a wind of deliverance by this man and that man, but as soon as they became prosperous again and set free from the oppressors, they began to sin, act carnally, every man doing what was right in his own eyes. They never had any character. How could they sustain the testimony of life that Israel should be? Only when a hero was raised up, when a preacher preached revival, then they suddenly got inspired, but there was nothing within—no discipline, no life. They could not carry it on.

The people of God have to learn at some point that the Lord is after a life, a Christ-inspired and Christ-strengthened life inside if His work is going to go on into fulness. Even the servants of God have to learn the lesson of Elijah, that there is a wind and there is a power but the Lord is not always in the wind. The still, small voice quickened his ministry. It is obedience to that still, small voice that perfects the ministry and must be heeded above the blowing and blustering and earthquakes and fires here and there (which was formerly Elijah's particular preference).

Now we have some people that hear the Lord's breath. In Zechariah 4:4 it says, "Not by might, nor by power, but by My Spirit, says the Lord." He breathes upon some people and they begin to hear this word; it is called *recovery.* They hear the Lord saying, "Listen, I have had enough of kings in the church. I have had enough of full-time servants, as it were. At best they can maintain the status quo, but that has not brought My people to fulness. I want to work by My Spirit in the inner man and produce a testimony whereby they will say, 'Grace, grace,' and not

'Thank God, it is brother so and so.'" So, the Lord raises up and begins to speak with His breath at the grass roots level to various people saying, "Will you obey Me? Will you take up My cross? Will you be faithful to Me? I don't care what the group is doing; will you overcome if you have to swim upstream from what the group is doing? You can do it by the power of My life within." And the Lord begins to raise up people who have this understanding that we need the life within.

People with such a burden are accused of being anti-charismatic. Well, if anti-charismatic means being against no discernment, carte blanche carryings on, then I suppose it is anti-charismatic; but nobody is anti-anything. The fact of the matter is that many people who are being called even now by the Spirit's speaking into their hearts are charismatic in background. It makes no difference. The Lord is not calling Charismatics or non-Charismatics. He is calling those who have an ear to hear: "I want the life of Christ in My church. I want My Son to have a bride. Who will obey and take up this discipline?" The Lord is doing that in His church today.

I have been a charismatic; I have been around charismatics and people in all kinds of dimensions in the Holy Spirit, and I can tell you with a clear conscience that I am not against the power of the Holy Spirit in any real manifestation. But I believe that the Lord, today, before the Lord comes back, is trying to cap the oil well of the Spirit to make this life of the Spirit fruitful, useful, and produce its desired effect.

I have been down to Houston a few times but I have never seen an oil well when it gushes out after they first strike oil. I have just seen that on television. When they strike oil, out comes the black gold, like the Beverly Hillbillies. They are all standing under it, hugging and saying, "We are rich, we are rich," and this black gold is falling on everybody. But the truth of the matter is, when that gusher goes, when the oil blows, it is probably forty percent water, fifteen percent gravel or sand, and all other kinds of impurities. You have got to cap that thing and then distill the oil in order to make it useful and powerful. The Lord does not want to take away the power of the Holy Spirit. In fact, the Spirit right now hovers, looking for vessels who have enough of the life of Christ that they can be trusted with an outpouring of the Holy Spirit. But He intends to cap it and not flaunt it. He is not around to show things off in ostentatious braggadocio, but rather to move by the power of the Spirit with people who can listen to His voice and also have the power of His anointing. It is the Lord's desire in this day. It is His heart. He is not saying, "No; no more power; it is too dangerous." It is the same Holy Spirit—the wind and the breath—and He will have both operating in the final day.

Now I want us to see this vital, two-fold ministry of wind and breath together. They can only be together. If they are taken apart and we become a windy group, we will go off the rails. But if we become a breathy group, we will die on the vine, weak, impotent, in-turned, introspective, sentimental, irrelevant, not witnessing to the world, hiding upstairs for fear of the Jews. Either way we lose, but this way the Lord can have fulness.

THE RELATIONSHIP OF THE WIND AND THE BREATH

With this idea in mind, I want to share three matters in this relationship of the wind and the breath. First, I want us to look at the historical significance of Pentecost because that is where the rushing wind began for the church. Secondly, I want us to try to understand the baptism in the Holy Spirit. Thirdly, I want us to see the ministry of the Holy Spirit in the church as both wind and breath.

THE HISTORICAL SIGNIFICANCE OF PENTECOST

First of all, as we look at Acts 2, we see Peter stand up and begin to proclaim his Pentecostal message. What is Peter basically saying? This rushing, mighty wind had come down upon those 120 believers. They began to speak in tongues and people gathered around and said, "What is going on here?" There were Galileans and a smattering of Judeans speaking in other languages. I am not sure if the other languages were just for their convenience so that they could understand what was being said, but the thing that captured them was that these were people under some influence. How were they suddenly so bold in their worship? In the synagogue the Jews would have worship and sing various songs, but they had never seen anything like this. Those dear brothers and sisters were lost in worship. They were magnifying God with a boldness that was scary. People said, "What is going on?" And Peter stood up and preached this sermon and said, "This is not drunkenness; this is what was promised in the book of Joel: 'In the last days I will pour forth My Spirit upon all flesh.'" And he began to share that message.

The Promise Given In The Old Testament

We need to look at the Old Testament background of Pentecost. Peter is saying, "What you are seeing now is the fulfillment of a prophesy given in Joel." What is this prophecy? First, this short book of Joel, from beginning to end, is a book whose prophetic theme regarded the day of the Lord—the coming back of the Lord Jesus. The "day of the Lord" is mentioned in Joel 1:15, 2:1, 2:11, 2:31, and 3:14. At the end of chapter 2, we have the Scripture that Peter was quoting from.

And it will come about after this that I will pour out My Spirit on all flesh; and your sons and daughters will prophesy, your old men will dream dreams, your young men will see visions, and even on the male and female servants I will pour out My Spirit in those days. And I will display wonders in the sky and on the earth, blood, fire, and columns of smoke. The sun will be turned into darkness, and the moon into blood, before the great and awesome day of the Lord comes. And it will come about that whoever calls on the name of the Lord will be delivered. (Joel 2:28-32)

Chapter 2 of Joel gives us a prophetic outline of the stages preceding the Messiah's coming. The first step had to do with the plague of locusts they were under which was seen as a judgment from God. The second stage began when the people cried out to God and He restored a remnant, filling their vats with wine and oil and restoring all the years the locusts had eaten. Then it says, "After this, sayest the Lord, I will pour out My Spirit upon all flesh."

"After this" means the third stage began after the restoration of the oil, vats and the years the locust had eaten.

The Sign of the Coming of the Lord

Stage three comes: "I will pour out My Spirit upon all flesh and your sons and your daughters will prophesy." What is Peter saying? He is saying that the pouring forth of the Spirit is a time marker for the day of the Lord. In other words, when you see the Spirit poured out upon all flesh, on all nations, you will know that the day of the Lord is coming soon. You will know the clock is ticking, counting down. When His Spirit is poured out, it is a sign that we are near the end. Basically, this is how the Jews understood it. When the Spirit is poured out upon Gentiles and anybody who calls on the name of the Lord can be saved, it means the end is very near. When children receive the Spirit and old people receive the Spirit and everybody who calls on the name of the Lord receives an out-pouring of grace from heaven by the Holy Spirit, it is a sign to Israel. This Joel 2 prophecy of the Spirit being poured out is a sign to Israel that the Messiah has begun to reign because the Spirit comes from the Messiah—the anointed One. *Meshiach* means "anointed one." Now, whenever Israel looked at the church, they saw a sign: "The Messiah has begun to reign." This was the Christian gospel on the day of Pentecost; but this was also a sign to the world. They said, "What is happening to these people? The Spirit is being poured out on them." And they said, "God is alive and He is the Savior of the world, and if you call on the name of Jesus Christ as Lord, you will receive this same Spirit." What a gracious gift! What a time-marker of the beginning of the end! What an important, historical marker. Understand; the church is a sign of judgment to Israel; the church is a sign that the end is coming soon; the church is a sign that the Messiah is reigning. And how does the church bear this sign? By the outpoured Holy Spirit. If the church does not have the Spirit upon it, it has no sign. This is the prophetic marker that the end is coming. But the church is more than that. This wind blowing, this mighty wind coming down and blowing marks the commencement of something more.

The Witnessing of the Resurrected Christ

The church is a sign of God's grace and favor and the outpoured Spirit for all nations. It is a sign that the end is soon to come and that the Messiah is reigning, but also, with the pouring forth of this wind there was a commencement of what is called "the witness." With the pouring forth of the Spirit, the witnessing to the resurrection of Christ began and we see this predicted in John 15:26: "I will send a Helper and He will bear witness of Me and so will you." In Acts 1:8 it says, "And you shall receive power when the Holy Spirit comes upon you and you shall be My witnesses." What does that mean? When you hear Acts 1:8, do you usually think of some Christian layman knocking on your door or handing out tracts on the street corners? Is that what it means to you to be a witness? When the disciples in Jerusalem heard this, they knew exactly where this phrase came from. It came from Isaiah. Let us look at it just to see what it means in the Old Testament to be a witness.

Isaiah 43:8-11—Bring out the people who are blind, even though they have eyes, and the deaf, even though they have ears. All the nations have

89

gathered together in order that the peoples may be assembled. Who among them can declare this and proclaim to us the former things? Let them present their witnesses that they may be justified, or let them hear and say, "It is true." "You are My witnesses," declares the Lord, and My servant whom I have chosen, in order that you may know and believe Me and understand that I am He. Before Me there was no God formed, and there will be none after Me. I, even I, am the Lord, and there is no savior besides Me.

Isaiah 44:6-8—Thus says the Lord, the King of Israel and his Redeemer, the Lord of hosts: "I am the first and I am the last, and there is no God besides Me. Who is like Me? Let him proclaim and declare it; yes, let him recount it to Me in order, from the time that I established the ancient nation. And let them declare to them the things that are coming and the events that are going to take place. Do not tremble and do not be afraid; have I not long since announced it to you and declared it? And you are My witnesses. Is there any God besides Me, or is there any other Rock? I know of none."

After rebuking and prophesying against Israel for her faithlessness, in Isaiah 41 the Lord says, "Be comforted, My people, watch what I am going to do." Then He holds court and says, "Okay, bring in all the gods of this world and their idols. Come in here and you witness to Me. Tell us of your great power; tell us what you can do. I have some witnesses and they will tell you who I am. Come on, tell us; tell us of your power, tell us of your might, tell us how you predict. Oh, you don't? That is right, because you are nothing. Speak, My witnesses, tell them about Me. I am the only God. Besides Me there is no other. There is no other Savior besides Me."

When Jesus said, "And when the power of the Holy Spirit comes upon you, you shall be My witnesses," this is what the disciples understood. They must testify that there is only one God and He is the living God. He is the only God and there is no other name given among heaven and earth by which man might be saved, except the name of Jesus. They were exclusive and they were adamant in their gospel preaching. You read it in Acts 2 and 3 or any one of the sermons that we have little bits of in the book of Acts. As you go through the book of Acts you see them standing against the god Artemis, the occult powers, they stood against Zeus and Hermes. Paul stood in the Arepagus and said, "Your gods are superstitions. Let me tell you of the one true and living God who made heaven and earth, and Jesus Christ who rose from the dead. There is no other name by which you may be saved." And they were convicted, cut to the quick under the impact of that kind of witness.

This is the history behind Pentecost. The Lord had commenced this worldwide witness, His Holy Spirit apostolically going out through the world bearing witness. Of course, He does not go by Himself; He uses human agency. There were men and women willing to stand up and bear this testimony and then the Holy Spirit came rushing behind with confirmation and with conviction. Sometimes, the disciples would preach a message and the Holy Spirit would do a miracle to confirm that this was true. Sometimes, the disciples would walk into a prayer meeting and the next thing you know a man was healed and so the Holy Spirit acted first. Then everybody said, "What's going on?" And the disciples had to explain: "Jesus is alive; that is what is going on. And if you repent this wind will come upon you, a season of refreshing from the presence of the Lord. Repent and know that the Messiah is alive." There was mighty preaching and mighty signs following.

THE BAPTISM IN THE HOLY SPIRIT

In this matter of the baptism in the Holy Spirit, which often proves to be controversial, let me say two things. I am sure that you have a view of what the baptism of the Holy Spirit is, and it may not be my view. I do not want to be controversial, and if you listen to what I have to say, I won't be controversial. But I do believe the Lord has shown me something in regard to this matter and I hope it helps in understanding what is going on.

The second thing I would say is this: A baptism is not some kind of release; a baptism is a straitening. When Jesus walked upon this earth, He said, "I have a baptism that I must be baptized with and I am straitened until it is accomplished" (see Luke 12:5). He was talking about His death. That is what a baptism always

93

symbolizes. He was always under the vision of the cross and it was straitening Him and pressing Him toward Jerusalem. He found no relief until He came out from under the restraint of that baptism. Now, the Holy Spirit lays hold of people and says, "Your life is not your own any longer; I have a mission for you." It is interesting how many people want to know the baptism of the Holy Spirit but how few of them are willing to give their lives to the Lord to be a witness for Him. I have a real conviction in my heart that there is a coordination between the receiving of power and the willingness to have your life laid down under the restraint and the moving of the Holy Spirit. At its deepest level, the baptism in the Holy Spirit is: Your life is not your own, you are under the lordship of the Holy Spirit. If He breathes and speaks, you listen to Him. If He sends you out, you listen to Him. He is the wind, He is the breath, He is your life. Are you willing for that?

As I have meditated on these things over these many years, my understanding is that the problem with our definitions of the baptism in the Holy Spirit is that basically they are too small. Let me take this phrase out of its theological phraseology and say "the immersion in the Holy Spirit." What does that picture to you? John the Baptist said, "I am immersing you in water for the forgiveness of sins but somebody is coming and when He gets hold of you, He is going to immerse you in the Holy Spirit." My understanding is that this is the marker of the age we now live in. Anyone who believes in Jesus Christ as Lord, our enthroned Lord Jesus Christ, takes you by His grace and plunges you into the Holy Spirit. He covers you outside, He fills you inside. He keeps you under so long you have to start breathing and take in the Holy Spirit. He indwells you. He comes in as a fire and begins to sanctify. Then Jesus says, "I love you," and He plunges you again, up and down, again and again, for the rest of our lives. Since the day of Pentecost, when the baptism in the Holy Spirit historically took place, its on-going effect is known in every believer. When you and I come to Jesus Christ and by grace are saved, He plunges us into the Holy Spirit and we get the whole load. That is what I think the baptism of the Holy Spirit means. It is a marker of the age. Listen to the context. It is only used seven times in the New Testament. Five times it is predictive; once in Matthew, once in Mark, once in Luke, once in John, and then in Acts 1. It is predicting what would happen. Then on the day of Pentecost, it happened, and in Acts 11, it is mentioned again as if looking back at the house of Cornelius when the Spirit fell and they said, "That is what happened back there." So we know what happened on the day of Pentecost. Its on-going effect is good until the end of this age. We are being immersed into the Holy Spirit. Thank God, we are being immersed in the Holy Spirit that we might know His power to serve and witness for the Lord, that we might know His voice speaking within, that we might know His indwelling life, that we might know His sanctifying power, and so forth.

FOUR MAJOR ASPECTS OF THE SPIRIT'S WORKING

There have always been, as I would group them, four major aspects of the Spirit's working, and there are people who define the baptism in the Holy Spirit in one of these four areas. Not many pick two. I have no argument with anybody. I believe it is all four of them. Let me explain.

Indwelling Life

Some people think the baptism in the Holy Spirit is when the Holy Spirit comes down into sinners and we are born again, and He indwells us with His indwelling life. He breathes on us; He quickens us; He brings us from death to resurrection ground. He begins to reveal the Scriptures. He speaks "Abba, Father" within us; it is the indwelling Holy Spirit. This is the unique work of the Holy Spirit in the New Testament era. In the past there had been outpourings of the Holy Spirit but there had never been the Holy Spirit living within you. G. Campbell Morgan says very clearly, "The baptism in the Holy Spirit is when you are born again and the Holy Spirit comes inside to dwell." I say "Amen." This is absolutely true.

Outpouring For Power

Some people say, "No, the baptism in the Holy Spirit is that outpouring for power." R. A. Torrey says, "It is a second experience. After you become a Christian, you surrender everything and you ask God to fill you with the Holy Spirit. He comes down and that is the baptism in the Holy Spirit. It is an outpouring of power for service. It is an anointing that enables you to be a witness and even to receive gifts as a servant in the body of Christ."

There are Charismatics of the same view that the baptism in the Holy Spirit is a second experience. The Holy Spirit comes down on you, you have some sensation, and you receive some gifts. I agree.

Sanctifying Experience

Some people say the baptism in the Holy Spirit is a sanctifying experience, the second blessing—John Wesley. They emphasize baptism in the Holy Spirit and fire, and when the fire of the Holy Spirit purges you and sets you free from sin that you have been struggling with, there is deliverance. Even though you are a Christian, there are sins you are not able to overcome and then, one day, the Holy Spirit comes down and touches your lips and sanctifies you and sets you free from sins. You do not become sinless. There are some who preach that heretical doctrine that you become sinless from then on. No; you are no longer under the bondage of sin. Some people call it the Galatians 2:20 experience. "I find that I am crucified with Christ and I do not have to struggle anymore. I have been sanctified, I have been set free somehow and His holiness begins to work itself into my life." I agree one hundred percent.

Incorporation Into the One Body

Some people say the baptism of the Holy Spirit is talking about the time when the Lord took 120 individuals and made them one body. He did an organic miracle and individuals were made one body. He gave birth to the church, and anybody who gets saved now He incorporates into the church as it says in I Corinthians 12, that by one Spirit you are baptized into one body. The Holy Spirit fits you in and gives you a home. You have a relationship, you have a place, you have a life in the body. You are incorporated into a living organism called the church. It is Jesus, the Head, putting you into His body. This is a miracle. I believe it one hundred percent.

EVERY CHRISTIAN BAPTIZED IN THE HOLY SPIRIT

I believe the baptism in the Holy Spirit is all four of those but here is what I think is important and this is where I stand. I believe every Christian has been baptized in the Holy Spirit. I am tired of hearing people say, "I have; you haven't." I do not buy it and I do not think it is Scriptural. Every Christian, born-again, has been baptized in the Holy Spirit and has as his inheritance an absolute right to the indwelling, the outpouring, the incorporation, and the sanctifying Holy Spirit all working in their lives. Once you become a Christian, this has happened. Your experience of these things varies from individual to individual and by the sovereign hand of the Holy Spirit, I might add. But I do not accept somebody saying that a Christian who has been bought with the same price has not been baptized in the Holy Spirit. Do you know why I believe that? Because the indwelling, the outpouring, the sanctifying work, and the incorporation are all in the finished work of Christ.

Let me make it as clear as I can to you by asking you four questions. Is it possible to be a Christian without the Holy Spirit dwelling in you? No. It says in Romans 8:9 if you do not have the Spirit dwelling in you, you do not belong to Christ. And if a man does not have that Spirit, we know this is true. This indwelling that was promised by Jesus—"He who has been with you will be in you"— was given when Jesus went away for a little while, dying on the cross and being raised again. We have the indwelling Spirit. Every Christian has the Spirit dwelling in him; otherwise, he could not be born again.

Do you know any Christians who are truly born again but they are not sure of their salvation? They have never heard the "Abba, Father" inside? Do you know some Christians who read the Bible but it does not speak to them even though they are born again and the Bible should speak to them? Do you know some Christians who are truly born again but they are not very clear of their conscience being really pricked regarding sin? The reason I am asking these questions is because we would like to think that everybody who is born again has the indwelling Holy Spirit, has the assurance of their salvation, opens the word and it is illuminated, they see revelations of Jesus and have the Holy Spirit speaking within as the voice, but I know many Christians who have not heard the voice speaking yet. When I deal with some teenagers, they come up to me and they say, "You know when I was saved? Well, my mom and dad prayed for me and I asked Jesus into my life when I was seven years old, but you know what? I do not know if I am a Christian."

I said, "Let's settle it right now. The Bible says he who has the Son of God has life. Do you have the Son of God?"

He would say, "Well, I don't know."

I said, "Did you ask Him to come into your life?"

He said, "Well, I believe so."

I said, "Let's make sure. Let's ask Him right now."

I have done this with so many teenagers, and they say, "Okay, Jesus, I want You in my life. I have wanted you ever since I was seven and I have prayed many times that You would come into my life." So I pray with them and afterwards, I say this: "Close your eyes one more moment. I want your soul to ask yourself, 'Jesus, do you live inside?'" And I will hear a kid break out in tears and say, "There He is; I heard Him, I heard Him." What a wonderful moment! And I say, "Do you know now He is inside you and you can say, 'Abba, Father'? My Father, my Father." It is an instantaneous understanding but they had to understand about the indwelling life and, suddenly, things began to come alive and the word of God opened up. It is true when they are saved they have this indwelling Spirit, but some people do not even know they have an indwelling Spirit. I know some Charismatic people who have gifts of the Holy Spirit and the power on them, yet they have no voice inside leading them, and they are doing everything carnally. I wish it were not so.

Is it possible to be a Christian and not have the outpouring of the Holy Spirit? Yes, that is possible; right? No; it is not because the outpouring is based on the finished work as well.

Peter said, "Jesus is enthroned in the heavens now; the Spirit has been poured out on you." It is based on the finished work that the Spirit is poured out on you and every Christian who has come into the good of the finished work has the outpoured Holy Spirit. But maybe you know some Christians who do not have boldness of witness, who do not seem to have power as they minister or try to serve Him. I think they need to hear that they already have something that is theirs to claim and receive. After the day of Pentecost, it is interesting to me, that the functional work that was asked of the church was not, "Have you been baptized in the Holy Spirit?" They never say that. They just say, "Have you received?" It implies that there is something already there for the taking. Now, have you received? May it be so!

Is it possible to be a Christian without the sanctifying touch of the cross in your life? No. When someone becomes a Christian, you can see that there is a sanctifying work, even external sanctifying work, a new moral energy to turn away from sins they could not turn away from before. But sometimes, it takes a while for this

Galatians 2:20 experience to happen, to be delivered from the power of haunting sin all the time. But it does not mean that they do not have it.

The same applies with being incorporated. The incorporation of our lives into the body of Christ happens at the moment of our salvation but some people have never heard that this is true. They are lone rangers out there as Christians, all by themselves. They do not think they have any place, there is no home, there is nowhere they fit in. Then they hear, "You are a functioning organ in the body of Christ. You belong to others and they belong to you." Something happens inside and they say, "I found my home." How wonderful it is when somebody finds his home in the house of God: "I fit in here."

Would to God we all experience these aspects of the Spirit's work because it is the same Holy Spirit. We cannot chop Him up into works. The power that comes down upon us is the same Holy Spirit who indwells and breathes within us. It is the same working Holy Spirit, and if we will follow the Lord and look to the Lord Jesus, we

will come into the richness of all these things. I
believe every Christian has been baptized in the
Holy Spirit.

NOT ALLOWING THE WIND TO OVERWHELM THE BREATH

I also have seen a second thing that has
become a conviction of mine. Would to God, all
of us could be a four-fold threat, but the reality is
that there is a richness in the body of Christ
which accrues when we stop trying to get other
people to be like us, when we truly believe they
all have the Holy Spirit and we start to see Christ
in them as the Holy Spirit operates. The fulness
that we need in the body of Christ is not every
Christian being a self-sufficient whole, operating
dimensionally and fully in all four of these areas.
But fulness comes when I am content to live with
saints where one perhaps has some anointing
and some power upon him and is able to
minister with power and boldness in evangelism
but maybe his nature needs some help right
now. Thank God, he has a brother who has
known by great experience the indwelling life.
The Spirit speaks to him and when he opens the

word, there is revelation. This brother with the power would give anything for the revelation this other brother sees. But the Lord has not given it that way so he is going to have to trust this brother.

Then you look at somebody else in the body of Christ and you say, "Man, whenever I see him, I see the beauty of holiness." It makes me want to say, "Jesus, plunge me into holiness. I want to be a partaker of holiness that I might see the Lord because I see Christ in this holy person." His life looks cut off and clean and beautiful. The Lord has done some deep, sanctifying work in this person's life. There is life; there is holy life.

Then we have some precious brothers and sisters, who, if they came up here to speak right now, would faint of nervous tension but they know their place in the body of Christ. They fit in and serve in such a precious way that we see Jesus, even if he is just the guy who shakes your hand when you come in the door, even if he is just the guy who is folding up the chairs in Jesus' name. But he knows his place and he fits so well. He encourages everybody to each side of him because he knows his place and he is not too much and he is not pretending he is too little. He is just there; he is incorporated. We live in a body like that.

But when we look at each other, based on our own experience, our temptation is to get narrow and say, "You need what I've got." So if we are Charismatics, we would look at the people and say, "What you need is power and boldness; get wet." And if you are a deeper life person, you look at the Charismatics and say, "Get character." The truth of the matter is, we have one another. Brothers and sisters, what a fulness we would have. But the problem is always this: The wind overwhelms the breath.

Of these four dimensions I mentioned, how many of them are breath and how many of them are wind? Maybe they are not so easy to define but we would certainly say that the outpouring is the wind. How about the sanctifying which is a deep work within? I would say that is breath. How about the indwelling? I would say that is breath. How about the incorporation? Well, it is a little bit of both but I think you have to go with breath. Now look at that; we have three to one in our population. How come the windbags run away with the show? I know, sometimes, I joke around and say things like that but I want to tell you something. Would to God that men who have the gift of ministry in their lives had brothers and sisters of the moral character to tell them to sit down and get their nature in order before they continue to minister. How it would have saved men who are now disgraced and ashamed of the body of Christ. But when we see a big windbag, we all fall back, and we dare not say anything. Oh, how they need some brother who has got enough character and grace to say, "Praise God for your ministry. Now, can I show you the more excellent way?" Apollos was really appreciative when Priscilla and Aquila came along by him and had enough of the life of Christ in them so they could say, "No, no, you need to understand some things." How we need one another so that we can have fulness. I do not ever want to see the wind and the breath apart. We truly need to walk together. And we need to stop expecting one another to be like us. We see too deep a mystery in the body of Christ.

I have seen some people (this is part of God's great humor) who do not believe in any gifts of the Holy Spirit. They believe they are all gone; yet the person operates in gifts of the Spirit. He says, "I do not believe in asking the Holy Spirit to fill my life. When I came to Jesus, He filled my life," and the Lord does. I also have seen in the mystery of the body of Christ a lot of people who think they have a gift and they don't.

FILLED WITH THE HOLY SPIRIT

I want to leave you with one picture from the New Testament that gives you an idea of what I have been seeing in this matter of fulness. We have these two phrases: "Filled with the Holy Spirit" and "Full of the Holy Spirit," and I think we should discern the difference. Almost all of the references to these two phrases are in the book of Acts. Six times filled is mentioned in the book of Acts: In Acts 2:4, on the day of Pentecost they were all filled with the Holy Spirit. In Acts 4:8 Peter stood up before the Sanhedrin and was filled with the Holy Spirit. In Acts 4:31 the church prayed and they were filled with the Holy Spirit. In Acts 9:17 Ananias says, "Paul, I have come to pray for you that you might be filled with the Holy Spirit." In Acts 13:9 Paul stands up before Elymas the magician and filled with the Holy Spirit brings him blindness. In Acts 13:52 the church, after persecution, was filled with joy and with the Holy Spirit.

These are the only six references in the Bible to being filled with the Holy Spirit. Most of the time they show some change of countenance, some boldness, some anointing coming upon Peter so that he could speak, and the hearers were able to take note of something in his countenance. Or Paul stands up and with a special authority takes hold of things; or the church, filled with this new boldness, goes out to witness. This is being filled with the Holy Spirit.

FULL OF THE HOLY SPIRIT

What does it mean to be full of the Holy Spirit? Being full denotes a state of things, and we find this four times in the book of Acts. In Acts 6:3 it says, "But select from among you, brethren, seven men of good reputation, full of the Spirit and of wisdom, whom we may put in charge of this task." In Acts 6:5 it mentions that

Stephen is full of the Holy Spirit. In Acts 7:55, as Stephen is about to be stoned, he is full of the Holy Spirit and sees the vision of heaven. In Acts 11:24, Barnabas is said to be a man full of the Holy Spirit.

Here is what I see as the difference. A man who is filled with the Holy Spirit is somebody who has had the Holy Spirit come upon him for ministry, service, or witness. A man who is full of the Holy Spirit is a man whose spirit within is under the control of the Holy Spirit, and so the river of the Spirit within meets the enclothing of the Holy Spirit upon. A man who is full of the Holy Spirit is a man with both character and an anointing of the Holy Spirit.

Whom would you choose to go and serve the widows? You wouldn't just choose somebody who has some gift of the Holy Spirit. You want a man of character, a man with wisdom, a man like Stephen or Barnabas or Philip. Such men have character. Their motives are right. In contrast, there are some people who have the gift of prophecy but they are not a prophet because they do not yet have the character of a prophet.

A man full of the Holy Spirit has the Spirit within and the Spirit without. This is a man full of the Holy Spirit. He knows the reality of the Spirit's wind but he is controlled by the breath of the Spirit within. May this be our portion in the church—men and women full of the Holy Spirit. May the Lord help us.

Let us pray:

Father, I can only speak from my heart in thanksgiving to You for all the ministrations that the Holy Spirit has borne into my life by the grace of the Lord Jesus and it leaves me with a two-fold response. I thank the Lord God that I have received all the portions of the Holy Spirit when I was saved through Jesus Christ. Thank You for the sanctifying work, thank You for the incorporation, thank You for the outpouring upon, and thank You for the indwelling. I thank You for it all and all You have given me. It is all my inheritance, all my down payment, and all of Your grace. Yet, within my heart there is a prayer: Oh Jesus, plunge me in some more. When I see a holy brother I say, "Oh Lord, I am willing to go through the cross to have such a testimony." When I see someone who has revelation, I say, "Oh God, plunge me into this indwelling life." When I see someone who has an anointing I say, "Oh Lord, pour down that Spirit from on high that I might be so bold with my witness." When I see someone fitting into the body, I say, "Oh Lord, strip me of my independence and plunge me in again until I find my place and fit in and am built together with the saints."

Oh Lord, You have put a hunger in my heart. Any invitation I will respond to. Lord, I want more of You and know the Holy Spirit's ministrations as the vehicle by which I might find and live in the name of Jesus Christ.

Lord, I pray that You take this message now, take any sting of controversy out of it. That is not at all the point, but may we learn, somehow, to abide and maintain the unity of the Spirit until we come to like understanding in the unity of an outworked faith, and in the meantime, appreciate what You are doing in one another, believing You have given full provision for everyone to be able to live the life of Christ here on this earth.

Oh, help us in this day to be a sign, to be a testimony that Jesus Christ is Lord and risen *again. Give us such a testimony–inside reality, outward anointing. Grant it to us, Lord, we pray in Jesus' name. Amen.*

THE BREATH

II Corinthians 4:7-18—But we have this treasure in earthen vessels, that the surpassing greatness of the power may be of God and not from ourselves; we are afflicted in every way, but not crushed; perplexed, but not despairing; persecuted, but not forsaken; struck down, but not destroyed; always carrying about in the body the dying of Jesus, that the life of Jesus also may be manifested in our body. For we who live are constantly being delivered over to death for Jesus' sake, that the life of Jesus also may be manifested in our mortal flesh. So death works in us, but life in you. But having the same spirit of faith, according to what is written, "I BELIEVED, THEREFORE, I SPOKE," we also believe, therefore also we speak; knowing that He who raised the Lord Jesus will raise us also with Jesus and will present us with you. For all things are for your sakes, that the grace which is spreading to more and more people may cause the giving of thanks to abound to the glory of God. Therefore we do not lose heart, but though our outer man is decaying, yet our inner man is being renewed day by day. For momentary, light affliction is producing for us an eternal weight of glory far beyond all comparison, while we look not at the things which are seen, but at the things which are not seen; for the things which are seen are temporal, but the things which are not seen are eternal.

John 13:33—Little children, I am with you a little while longer. You shall seek Me; and as I said to the Jews, I now say to you also, 'Where I am going, you cannot come.'

John 14:1-4—Let not your heart be troubled; believe in God, believe also in Me. In My Father's house are many dwelling places, if it were not so, I would have told you, for I go to prepare a place for you. And if I go and prepare a place for you, I will come again, and receive you to Myself; that where I am, there you may be also. And you know the way where I am going.

John 14:16-17—And I will ask the Father, and He will give you another Helper, that He may be with you forever; that is the Spirit of truth, whom the world cannot receive, because it does not behold Him or know Him, but you know Him because He abides with you, and will be in you.

John 15:1—*I am the true vine, and My Father is the vinedresser.*

John 15:4—*Abide in Me, and I in you. As the branch cannot bear fruit of itself, unless it abides in the vine, so neither can you, unless you abide in Me.*

John 16:16-18—*A little while, and you will not longer behold Me; and again a little while, and you will see Me. Some of His disciples therefore said to one another, "What is this thing He is telling us, 'A little while, and you will not behold Me; and again a little while, and you will see Me'; and, 'because I go to the Father'?" And so they were saying, "What is this that He says, 'A little while'? We do not know what He is talking about".*

We have spoken about the Holy Spirit being as the wind and the breath in His ministry. He is the wind of power moving the church, witnessing the gospel, performing wonders as He worked upon the church, bringing revelation to the people of God and molding them together.

We also understand that He is the breath. He is inside of us. He is the very life that springs forth in living waters. He is the One that we need every hour just as much as we need to take a breath. And so the Scriptures exhort us again, "Be filled with the Spirit."

It is unfortunate that because of misunderstandings regarding who the Holy Spirit is and His activity, this is an exhortation that causes Christians difficulty. It should not. To be plunged into the Holy Spirit is to be plunged into the Lord Jesus and into God Himself. To know Him and His enabling, His equipping, His power, and His leading is indeed a blessing of blessings. To know His life within is not only our salvation but it is the hope of glory. His work will be faithfully done in us in such a way that we will be presented perfect unto the Lord Jesus Christ at His coming again.

I really pray that when you hear this exhortation, "Be filled with the Holy Spirit," you will not have any check, any hesitancy as to what He is saying , but instead will say, "Yes, Lord; fill me within and without. Incorporate me into the body of Christ so I know my place, just where I fit."

As we consider now this matter of the *breath,* we know that so much of this communion of the Spirit goes on in the background, as we have said, united in our spirit, breathing words to us, uniting us to the Lord Jesus and co-working with Him in this new dwelling place within. It is corporate as well, as He works in the body in His own mysterious way when we gather together. It is not so easy to see Him (since He is breath), but we know His work and are truly dependent upon that work. We see in the order of II Corinthians 13:14, that the grace of the Lord Jesus comes first. It is certainly the doorway into the experience of the reality of the Godhead. Beyond our talk of God's eternal purpose and counsels and all manner of visions, the fact of the matter is that we need to live in the presence of God— Father, Son, and Holy Spirit. This is, in fact, the eternal purpose and design of God.

We shared about the wind that began to blow at Pentecost and the wind's mission--the sign of the outpoured Spirit upon the church signaling that the end is near and the day of the Lord is about to be. We saw the wind blowing, ushering in this present era of witnessing foretold in Isaiah where the church testifies to the only true and living God and the fact that He alone can save. This was communicated by the apostles throughout the then known world by the preaching of the gospel, and the Holy Spirit went behind them with great power and confirmation.

The book of Acts is actually a history over a number of years, so we should not think that the apostles and the Christians walked in manifested miracles every day. But they preached the gospel faithfully and there was, in fact, a miracle that attended every preaching of the gospel. The convicting work of the Holy Spirit, behind the gospel preaching, spoke into the hearts of those who heard these things. As the gospel was preached the Holy Spirit breathed into hearts, "These things are true; these things are true." He was a blowing wind and a convicting breath.

He stills blows today. He raises up a group of people, pours out His grace, His anointing and power, and gets them going. People come to the

Lord, and these seasons of grace are such a wonderful wind of refreshing. But as we have said, historically, the church eventually comes to a point where the wind needs to touch the breath, where the indwelling Holy Spirit, the voice speaking within and producing the character of Christ, needs to be developed among the saints in such a way that the wind does not just lead them off the rails. It is not the Holy Spirit who leads someone off the rails but there can come along many substitute winds that have the same feeling as the power of the Holy Spirit. There is an empowering on the body and the soul that happens when the Holy Spirit's power comes down upon us. We manifest an amazing sensitivity of mind and a power of emotion and will under this anointing, and even our bodies are quickened with power.

But as you know, evil spirits can come upon someone with similar effect and we must not be naïve in thinking Christians can easily tell the difference. They can even come like an angel of light. John is straight forward in saying, "We need to test the spirits." If we do not have clarity as to the anointing within, if we cannot hear the

Holy Spirit inside of us saying "Wait a minute, something is wrong here," we are liable to fall into mixture, deception, and many such things. Then when the Holy Spirit's wind has long since passed, man's own soulish wind keeps on blowing. Ministers can be great bags of wind, sometimes exercising so much power, and yet doing all kinds of dreadful things. The Lord pours out His Spirit, giving gifts unto men, but if He remains a carnal man, great damage can be done by his empowered soul.

However, if a man will learn the lessons of the Holy Spirit's anointing within—learn to hear the voice, learn to embrace the cross, learn when to go and when to stay, learn that his ministry is not more important than his life—then his power will be a valuable thing to the Lord. His character needs to be kept and treasured and guarded by the Holy Spirit within. If a man is willing to learn these kind of lessons, then the anointing can come without ill effect. As a matter of fact, such a one has a greater anointing because, as it were, there is an anointing of rivers coming up from within, and there is an anointing coming upon. This integration of the outward anointing with an inward discerning applies corporately to the church as well. So there comes a point, a crossroad, where from the outward understanding of Christianity with its grace and love and feeling, we have to go on to maturity.

I remember when I was first saved at the age of twenty, when I prayed, my hair used to stand up on my arms. I just felt the presence of God and all such wonderful, though external things. But the point comes in the Christian life, if we are to go on to maturity, that we have to live by the life within and not be dependent on feelings and anointings and words and external things. These have a place in the body of Christ but nothing can replace what the Lord has intended: that you and I, each one in this new covenant, know the Lord ourselves. We have His word written in our hearts. We know the commandment of God, and the Lord can lead us not only by wind but by breath. This is the same Holy Spirit. So let's not chop Him up and say, "Throw out the wind; we want the breath." It does not work. It is the same Holy Spirit.

EXPERIENCING THE INNER REALITY OF THE LIFE OF CHRIST

Now we come to this transition, moving from the outward to an understanding of the inward reality of the Spirit's work. We talked about the grace of our Lord Jesus, the love of God, and the communion of the Holy Spirit. These can just be understood externally until, inwardly, we begin to experience their reality by the communion of the Holy Spirit. He fellowships the things of Christ and brings us into their inner reality.

We can see the Lord helping the disciples make this transition in John 13-17. They have been used to walking with Jesus, depending on Him telling them where to go, depending on Him for their strength and anointing. Then in chapter thirteen Jesus arrests their attention by saying, "I said to the Jews that where I am going you cannot go, now I say to you, 'Bye, bye.'" He had gotten their attention: "Wait a minute, what do You mean? What is happening?" Then Jesus, in this precious last discourse, began to change their understanding of life from an external to an internal.

Jesus said, "I am going but I am preparing a place for you in the Father's house. This house is not the temple or a synagogue or even a geographical location. You know this house; you will be in it soon. I'm going to prepare it for you." He cannot just be talking about when we die and go to heaven. Based upon this verse in the King James version it would seem everyone has a mansion there. We use these verses for comfort at a funeral. But in the Greek the phrase is "abidings" or "dwellings." He is creating these for us by going away and then we can dwell there with Him and the Father. He said: "I am leaving, but I am coming back in a little while and My Father's house is going to be yours. But you are going to have to understand that this is a house not made with hands. I am not trying to build another institution, organization, religion. There is an organic house here." Is there any doubt He is speaking of the church?

Then in a second reorienting word He said, "I have been your strength, I have been your comforter, and I have been your teacher. Now I am going away but I will be coming back to you in a different way. I will dwell inside of you. You will no longer have to say, 'Where is Jesus? We have to ask Him a question.' You will have a teacher within. I am sending another Comforter. You are not going to get comfort from finding Me anymore in the physical body but from my voice speaking from within. The Spirit that has been with you and will be in you. You will still find your strength, your resource for ministering and life by abiding in Me. I am going away but you can still abide in Me and I will abide in you; I am still your vine, I am still your life. Abide in My word and you will bear fruit. Abide in My commandments and You will know My love. Abide in My love and you will be complete. You will do works, you will do much work, and as you abide in Me, I will prune you, and I will enable you to bear witness. You will see."

They said, "How can we abide in You? Where are You going? What is happening? Why are You leaving us? Where is the Father's house?" They were used to Jesus in the flesh. They did not know about the house to be built of living stones. Then Jesus said, "You will understand in a little while." They did not understand the significance of *the little while*. "What is He saying, *a little while?* And why did He just undo our whole lives? He has told us that He is going away, yet He is still going to be here. We have a house but it is not in Galilee or Jerusalem. We do not understand."

THE WORK OF THE CROSS AND RESURRECTION

What happened in the "little while" that opened the disciples' viewpoint to an inward understanding of life? The cross, the resurrection, and Pentecost. After Jesus died on the cross and rose again, He came to them, and the next thing you know they began to see the house and they began to sense the Holy Spirit within leading, guiding, enabling. For example, at Pentecost Peter stood up and spoke in the power of the Holy Spirit. John could have stood up but the Spirit had Peter stand up and the eleven stood with him, and you know the story. The Spirit revealed Old Testament Scriptures in their application to the Messiah.

The Holy Spirit also began bringing to remembrance things that Jesus said. In John 2 it says that after the resurrection, they understood what Jesus meant about "this temple" being destroyed and in three days coming back up. Rockets were going off within them by revelation. Can you imagine the early days there in the church and the things they started to discover? They said, "How come, brother, I feel so close to you? I did not even know you. Besides, you are a Hellenistic Jew and I am from Palestine or from Galilee. How can we love one another? There is something going on here." They had not yet heard Paul's lingo about body life at that moment, but they were experiencing these things as the Holy Spirit began to internalize these truths that had been heard on the outside. This is why the fellowship of the Holy Spirit is so precious to us. He grabs hold of our hands on some truth and takes us through a cross, a burial, and a resurrection into the reality of the very thing that was just a theory.

THE PROBLEM IN THE CORINTHIAN CHURCH

To see the importance of this inward reality we will be looking at Paul's letters to Corinth. The church at Corinth knew the Holy Spirit's wind upon them, but there was a lot more work that needed to be done by the fellowship of the Holy Spirit because the Corinthians, as a whole, remained outward in their viewpoint. They looked on the outer man in just about every way. This made them babes, and even though the grace of the Lord Jesus and the love of God and the communion of the Holy Spirit was theirs to have, they did not abide in these things because they had an outward view of things.

Corinth was a university center and full of Greek knowledge. Those brothers and sisters liked knowledge, they liked philosophy, they liked human wisdom, and it was preventing them from seeing the things which eye has never seen nor ear heard nor heart understood. Paul said, "I have a wisdom to tell you but you are still like babes and you are dependent on human wisdom. You are seeing things externally, and the Holy Spirit has some things to show you internally. You need the cross. When I came to you, what did I preach? Wisdom? I preached the cross. If you ever let go of your human wisdom, you will start entering into a spiritual wisdom by the Holy Spirit's fellowship with you, but right now you are looking at the outside."

"First, you have this outward view of ministry. So you prefer this apostle because he shares three points and a poem. Then some of you like that apostle because he is a fisherman and you like the way fishermen are, just rugged, good men. You are looking at this whole thing outwardly. Look at it inwardly. Who are we? We are gardeners—some plant the seed and some water it. But what is the big deal here? The Lord uses all of these different gardeners to make the garden grow, so why are you choosing and saying, 'We just want the water pot guy'?"

Then Paul says to the Corinthians: "You have a very Greek, tolerant view of this whole matter of people sinning in your midst, such as this man who is living with his father's wife. You are very laid back and worldly about it. You do not even see the real issue, the leaven of immorality that is going through the whole church. You do not even see that, do you?"

Then you are suing people, saying, 'I've got my rights, I've got my rights.' You do not realize you are ruining the testimony of the church which should be able to pray and find an answer to these disputes together. There should be spiritual wisdom in the body. Why isn't it there? What is wrong? Why are you such babes? This is all external stuff."

"You are saying, 'The gift makes the Christian. I've got the gift of prophecy; I am better than the guy who just speaks in tongues.' Don't you know the truth is that love should mark the Christian not the gift?"

"Then some of you say, 'Well, I've got a conscience and I don't like the way you are eating that meat.' Others say, 'I have knowledge. I know better; idols don't fool me; they don't scare me. I know there is no such thing as those idols.' Where is the man who has love and denies his eating rights in order not to offend his brother?"

"Then there is someone who thinks he is better than the other guy because he has some knowledge that another does not have. 'I have a revelation; you do not have a revelation. I am bigger than you are.' Where is this love that embraces everybody? What is the matter here? You are just looking at things outwardly."

By the time Paul writes II Corinthians we find that things have not gotten much better. Throughout this book, in one way or another, Paul has to defend himself from some detractors that have raised up saying that Paul is not really very good in ministry. In II Corinthians 5:12-13 he said, "We are not again commending ourselves to you but are giving you an occasion to be proud of us, so that you will have an answer for those who take pride *in appearance* and not in heart."

Those Corinthians should have been able to look into the heart of Paul and see the legitimacy of what he was doing; that his motives and his conscience were clear. But because they were looking at outward credentials and measuring him by ministerial standards such as rhetorical ability or demonstrative powers, Paul had to say, "Why are you just looking at the outward appearance?"

We have this same problem noted again in II Corinthians 10:7. As he takes up this matter of his apostleship in earnest, we find him saying, "You are looking at things as they are outwardly.

If anyone is confident in himself that he is Christ's, let him consider this again within himself, that just as he is Christ's, so also are we." You are looking at things outwardly.

THE NEED FOR REVELATION

If the Lord is going to make His love, His grace, and His wisdom an abiding reality and blessing in our lives, we have got to allow the Holy Spirit to communicate and fellowship Christ with us in such a way that He brings an inward perspective of these things. Paul even said that even in tribulations we "...must look, not at the things which could be seen, but at the things that cannot be seen, because the things that can be seen are temporal but the things that cannot be seen are the eternal things." Seeing the important things need this kind of vision to see them. The key to prayer and intercession is to see the unseen and not be so preoccupied with the seen stuff. This is Paul's life. He is a spiritual man. He has come to the place where the grace and the love and the fellowship of the Spirit are a living reality for him.

The Holy Spirit wants to minister the reality of things to us. In Paul's prayer in Ephesians 1:17, he said, "I pray that you might have the spirit of wisdom and revelation in the knowledge of Christ." This revelation of Christ is the basis of transitional seeing. Then he mentions three things that can be understood externally in their doctrine or internally in their reality.

First Paul prayed, "I want your eyes to be opened that you might see what is the hope of His calling." How many of you know that you can think of *calling* in an external way? What is my calling? What is my job? Tell me about that.

The second thing Paul wanted them to see by revelation was His inheritance in the saints. We can look at the saints as being problems where we live or we can see them through a revelation of Jesus Christ. The point the Holy Spirit always brings us back to is in seeing Jesus Christ in relationship to every area of your Christian life— whether its your calling, the saints, or even His power—these three things Paul prayed about.

Thirdly, do we see power externally? We can say, "Thank God, I have got the power; I have got the anointing. You need to get the anointing; let me pray for you." But no; by revelation in Jesus Christ we see His power—such incredible power welling up—the same power by which He was resurrected from the dead and seated at the right hand of God. This power is in relationship to Jesus, and not just to some separate, external force that we use as Christians. Every area of our life—our calling, relationships, and power—need to be brought under the feet of Jesus Christ and seen in relationship to Him.

THE WORKING OUT OF THE REVELATION INTO REALITY

The Holy Spirit within you enables you to see the revelation, and then the He walks you through and into the reality. This revelation leads to a walk that runs right through Ephesians. First, we must see what is the hope of His calling. By the way, the term *His* calling has no mistake in its pronoun. Paul is saying that first you need to see your calling in relationship to His calling. Then, in chapter 4:1, he says, "Let us learn how to walk worthy of the calling with which we have been called." Our calling is in relation to His calling. If we do not see the revelation of His calling as King of kings and Lord of lords, as Groom, as the Messiah, and all of these things, then we will not see our calling. We should not be thinking, "What is my job?" Oh, there is something so much more here! We are representatives of the King. If we see His calling, it immediately ennobles us. Then we realize, "I have got to walk worthy of this now. I am a servant of Jesus Christ; now that is an important job. I have seen Jesus." Suddenly, our calling takes on a nobility.

When we see the Lord Jesus and how He loves the saints, even the common saints where we live, it will cause us to say, "If Jesus loves them so much, they must be valuable. I better take another look." I take another look and I start to see that they are the rich inheritance of Christ. Jesus says, "I love the saints in your fellowship." So I need to start looking at them in a different way. We see the Holy Spirit taking us by the hand through chapters 4 and 5, walking us through it and announcing, "Now, submit to one another; submit to that treasure." We see the revelation and He walks us through it. Does it involve some of our cross? Maybe? Just a little bit?

And then in this matter of power we cry, "Oh, I want the power. I want to serve God. I want the power." Then He says, "Let's exercise power under My headship doing spiritual warfare as in chapter 6. Let's learn how to use that power and prevail before God's throne." Now, that is not quite so outwardly rewarding and exciting because He gets the glory and I don't. So the Lord says, "You need the cross; let Me walk you through this." Anybody who is a veteran in spiritual warfare does not have much left to brag about. The enemy has shot off most of their loose appendages, but they sure do trust in Jesus.

THE INNER MAN PREPARED FOR CHRIST TO DWELL

In Paul's prayer in Ephesians 3 we will just look at two verses in the middle of this long prayer: "That He would grant you, according to the riches of His glory, to be strengthened with power through His Spirit in the inner man, so that Christ may dwell in your hearts through faith" (Ephesians 3:16-17a).

This is such a precious verse. In chapter 1, he says that the Holy Spirit wants to reveal Jesus Christ in every dimension of our lives. Then in chapter 3, the Holy Spirit is working inside the manhole of our life, strengthening our inner man so that Christ can dwell there. He wants Jesus in our lives. He strengthens us; He fortifies our inner man by showing us who we are in Christ. He renews our mind. We begin to understand that we love holiness and righteousness, and He fills us with love. He sanctifies us, stripping some things from us, and He continues to strengthen our conscience so that we can stand firm when the enemy accuses us. He increases our spiritual sensibilities as we begin to hear His voice. The Lord wants to dwell in our hearts but there has to be a work done there, a resurrected reconstruction, as it were, strengthening the inner man so that Christ can dwell there safely. It cannot be an inner man that collapses every other day—alive today because we are in a conference and then deflating like a balloon for another year. Our inner man needs strength to know he has been born again by the grace of the Lord Jesus and can be faithful and grow in the word, in revelation, in the life, and all these things. So the Holy Spirit indwells and says, "Let's build here." This is the communion of the Holy Spirit, building our lives so that Christ can dwell, revealing Christ, and relating every aspect of our life to Christ.

THE GOD OF ALL COMFORT

Now we want to concentrate on this matter of the fellowship of the Holy Spirit as it is presented throughout II Corinthians. In I Corinthians Paul says, overtly, to those who have this outward view: "You need to know the cross and its working in your life." But in II Corinthians, actually, there is only one reference to the words *crucified* or the *cross* and that is in chapter 13. Yet, we can see how the fellowship or communion of the Holy Spirit is being worked out in Paul's life as he goes through the various ups and downs of his life and ministry. When we look at Paul in II Corinthians, we see someone who is being worked upon and who has been worked upon by the Holy Spirit. You see the cross and the resurrection everywhere. We want the fellowship of the Holy Spirit, or so we say, but do you know that when you first meet Him, you meet Him at the cross? If you hang in there, you will come out on the other side in resurrection life and with more of Christ in you. This is the fellowship of the Holy Spirit.

Sometimes, when we think of the fellowship of the Comforter we say, "Oh, praise God; He comforts me, He meets my needs, He loves me, He helps me, He does many comforting things in my life. Oh, I want the Comforter to come and comfort me." Unfortunately, this old word *comforter* which is used in the King James does not mean what we think it means. The word *comforter* is "paraclete" in the Greek. In chapter 1 of II Corinthians he talks about the God of all comfort: "Blessed be the God and Father of our Lord Jesus Christ, the Father of mercies and God of all comfort, who comforts us" (II Corinthians 1:3-4a). Here we are, comfortably comfortable. When we think of comfort, we just automatically feel comfortable.

The original word *comforter*, as it was used in King James' days, meant somebody who comes with fortification, as in fort, to strengthen, to fortify with. The Holy Spirit comes and strengthens you and gives you courage. You are going through a tough time and the Holy Spirit comes but He does not say, "Oh, too bad. I feel so bad for you, you little pussycat; have a little milk." Oh no; He comes into you and says, "Is anything impossible for the Lord? Do you really trust in Him? You can trust Him. I'll stand with you. We are here together; we will find the Lord in this thing." You sense that strength and know it is the Lord's strength. That is the comfort that comes. Sometimes it can be the comforting of a broken heart as we use the word comfort, but it is always a strengthening. *Paraclete* is a Greek word that means: "He comes alongside of us." So Paul says, "Let's bless the God who comes alongside of us." In all of our tribulations He comes alongside.

TROUBLE PRECEDES COMFORT

Now here is how it works. This is the formula, and we find it in II Corinthians 1:3-7.

This process of strengthening, comforting, coming alongside, or communion of the Holy Spirit usually starts when we are in trouble. If you want communion, you are heading for trouble. You will all have trouble and afflictions. The Greek word for tribulation is *thlipsis* and means "pressure." It does not necessarily mean persecution. It can be, but it means pressure, a squeezing. That is where it starts. The Lord has to get our attention. We do not tend to grow when things are easy. It is just like the disciples. If Jesus had not said "I am going away," they would have never said, "Wait a minute, what about..." They would have never been open to the revelation of His abiding life. Therefore, what happens to us is that trouble comes along. Now, there is a cross within the trouble. Many times the trouble is not the cross but the trouble squeezes an issue out in our life that needs the cross.

The second part of this process, after affliction comes along, is the Holy Spirit coming alongside and saying, "Okay, first of all, I want you to know that I am with you going through this." If that does not strengthen you, I do not know what can.

When Paul looked back in Philippians 3:10 he said, "I found two avenues of really getting to know the Lord. One is in the power of His resurrection. When I see Him working by resurrection life, I see Jesus every time. The other thing is in the fellowship of sufferings. In II Corinthians 1:5 it says, "For just as the sufferings of Christ are ours in abundance, so also our comfort is abundant through Christ." Do we want to get to know the Lord? Then, the next time you have trouble, the next time you have pressure, bring the Lord into the thing. The Comforter wants to come alongside. Say to Him, "Oh Comforter, strengthen me, encourage me, help me understand what is going on. Show me the issues here. Get me through this thing."

Then, of course, part three of the process is that He gets you through it; but as He takes you through this process, He both takes something away from you and adds something to you. There is something of the outward that needs to go. As Paul put it, "I have this treasure in an earthen vessel;" so the Lord has to break off another piece of the vessel so the treasure will shine. He breaks off a bit of the outward and adds something in your heart that He has worked into you through His fellowship of Christ.

Now that you have been through the trouble, it turns out, maybe as a surprise, that there are other people who have similar troubles that you can now comfort. Because the Holy Spirit has fellowshiped with you through the problem and brought more of Christ to you somehow in your life in a constituent way, you can fellowship with somebody else who has trouble and you can bring life to them by saying, "Listen, I have been through that. Now, let's stand together and ask the Lord to be with you and bring you through that." This is what Paul talks about here in verse 6: "If we are afflicted, it is for your comfort and salvation and if we are comforted, it is for your comfort also." We understand that we are going through these afflictions together. As a matter of fact, it brings about a confidence. This is one of those paradoxical realities of the Christian life— the more trouble you go through with the Lord, the more confident you are that He will use it for good.

In II Corinthians 1:7, Paul says, "Through our tribulations and through your tribulations our hope for you is firmly grounded, knowing that as you are sharers of our sufferings you are sharers of the comforts." When we hear that you are going through trouble, we pray for you but we know you are going to come out on the other side with more of Jesus realized in your life, a deposit of Jesus that cannot be snatched away. " So we say, "Cross, do its work. Resurrection, bring His life." This is the fellowship of the Holy Spirit. Life increases to others and we learn lessons as He inwardly abides in us and we see the Lord.

PAUL'S AFFLICTIONS

This is the theory, you might say, but Paul gives us an example, immediately, to show exactly what he is talking about. He goes on in verse 8 and says, "For we do not want you to be unaware, brethren, of our affliction which came to us in Asia, that we were burdened excessively, beyond our strength, so that we despaired even of life." Paul went through trouble and afflictions so bad that he was burdened excessively, which means, more than he had ever been before. His strength was completely stripped in this trouble. He despaired even of his life. That is how bad the trouble was.

We sometimes despair of life when we don't get our IRS refund check. But Paul was in such a pit of controversy, persecution, who knows what he means? Are these the lions in Ephesus? Is this his persecution? We do not know exactly what this trouble was in Asia. It is probably more than he even listed in chapter 11 when he listed some of the things he went through; but we know he went through a tough, tough time. Nevertheless, the Lord came by his side in this trouble. Notice what it says in verse 9: "Indeed, we had the sentence of death within ourselves in order that we should not trust in ourselves, but in God who raises the dead."

THE LESSON PAUL LEARNED

Something was learned and Paul says it was that as he despaired of life, he received an impression within and it was this: "You know

Paul, you have the sentence of death on your own self-reliance. You cannot trust your own self-reliance, you cannot trust yourself. You have used all your wits." Maybe he tried using his Roman citizenship. It did not work. Or maybe he used his influential Christian friends: "See if you can talk to someone and stop this problem." It did not work. Maybe he used his wits, his personality, his bravery, everything he could, and nothing worked.

The Lord said, "I am coming alongside, Paul, and I want to take away something that is very dear to you. It is your own wits and self-reliance. You cannot rely on that here, Paul; there is the sentence of death on that thing (You know when you are relying on yourself, it is a pretty 'iffy' situation anyway). Now I want to give you something you can rely on all the time. It is the resurrection life of Jesus Christ. I want you to trust the resurrection life to the point where you say, 'If my life is over; I will be resurrected. I am just going to trust a God who can resurrect and who can take something that is dead and make it come alive again.'" There is that part of Christ that got into Paul through his tribulation or was reaffirmed, as I am sure it was many times in Paul's life. As he came to the end of himself, he found that he could trust in resurrection life and then, it says, the Lord delivered him: "Who delivered us from so great a peril of death, and will deliver us" (v. 10).

Once you trust in the resurrection life, your confidence that God will deliver you is buoyant. It is invincible; what can they do to me? Even if they kill me, I still win. This is a win-win situation. I can trust that resurrection life. Somehow, this was brought into his life, and with that trust, confidence grew in him. That gave him the encouragement to go on to the next place of ministry because he realized: "He will deliver me again because my deliverance is not based on my wits anymore; it is based on the promise of resurrection."

While Paul was going through this something else happened to him. While he was praying and waiting, with nothing more he could do, he realized what he needed. He was so thankful the saints were praying for him. He was comforted by that. He was thanking God that those saints were praying for him. He says, "I trust that He on whom we have set our hopes will deliver us." In verse 11 he said, "You also joining in helping us through your prayers, so that thanks may be given by many persons to God for His grace in this deliverance." Paul knew the Lord had worked something else wonderful into him. He realized his interdependence on those intercessory people. When he was relying on himself, he was not so aware of that but now the Holy Spirit made him say, "Thank you, Corinthians. Thanks for praying for me because you helped bring me through." He had to depend not only on the resurrection power of the Lord Jesus but he could not do anything unless the saints were praying for him.

What happened to Paul? A little bit of the earthen vessel got chipped away but you see more treasure there now. Paul was more alive with the Spirit than he ever was before. He says, "You know, my old body can decay but my spirit is being renewed more every day I go through this fellowship with the Holy Spirit. He is teaching me new and wonderful things about

Jesus—faithful Jesus, resurrected Jesus, my Guide and Comforter, blessed God."

Paul's letters to the Corinthians themselves are examples of the fellowship of the Holy Spirit. When Paul wrote letters, he did not just write letters; he fellowshiped the Lord Jesus. That is the fellowship of the Holy Spirit because Paul is a man in Christ. We see in his letters an illustration of how the Holy Spirit wants to fellowship with us.

THE VIOLATION OF PAUL'S FELLOWSHIP WITH THE CORINTHIANS

You know the history of what happened to Paul in relation to the Corinthians. He sent the letter of I Corinthians as a letter of correction along with many other things. Afterward he went through Corinth briefly at some point in his ministry. He was just passing through but there was a problem; he was not received well. There was something going on there that caused him to leave and it was a bad experience. He says so in II Corinthians 2:1, "But I determined this for my own sake, that I would not come to you in sorrow again." This is what he was saying: "Do you want to know why I have not come by and visited? Do you remember how I said I would come by and see you on my way but I did not come by? Do you want to know why? The last time I came by after sending you I Corinthians, there was something wrong, and I just could not come by until something was straightened out."

There is a cost to real fellowship and it is this: We need to share Christ with one another in the light and with a clear conscience. If we are in the light as He is in the light, we have fellowship one with another, and the blood of Jesus Christ cleanses us from sin. But if there is an outward issue that causes their heart not to be open to Paul, then there is a problem. How can we openly share Christ one with another? Now if you have something against me we can be outward in our fellowship and say, "Hey, how is everything going?" "Fine, how is everything with you?" "Great, praise God, okay." But real fellowship senses the violation inwardly. So Paul had to write a very strong and difficult letter. In 2:4 we read, "For out of much affliction and anguish of heart I wrote to you with many tears; not so that you should be made sorrowful, but that you might know the love which I have especially for you."

Then he sent this letter off with Titus: "Titus, take this letter to the Corinthians and come back and tell me how things are." He wrote a difficult letter. He said a little later on, "After I sent that letter I had second thoughts. I regretted for a moment sending that letter but then I said, 'No, I have got to be truthful; I cannot have fellowship unless I am truthful. I have got to share my conscience. There is something violated here and there is something that is wrong.'" After Paul sent that letter he agonized and agonized and agonized. He waited to hear from Titus as we see in verses 12-13: "I came to Troas for the gospel of Christ and when a door was opened for me in the Lord, I had no rest for my spirit, not finding Titus my brother; but taking my leave of them, I went on to Macedonia."

He was so troubled he could not even preach the gospel in Troas. He struggled; he was in agony; he was waiting to hear. In II Corinthians 7:5 he said, "For even when we came into Macedonia our flesh had no rest, but we were afflicted on every side: conflicts without, fears within." Paul was going through agony. This agony, as he explained later, was over the Corinthians. He loved them, but he sent them this tough letter; he had to be truthful in Christ. He had not heard from them and he was agonizing and he was praying: "Oh God, don't let that letter be misunderstood. Don't let it cause any kind of division that the enemy could use." He was just in agony.

The Holy Spirit wants to reveal Christ to us so much. He wants to strengthen our inner man so much, but sometimes, there is an outward issue that is blocking our fellowship with the Holy Spirit. It may be our reliance on ourselves, a sin we are hiding from, but there is something preventing our fellowship with the Holy Spirit. He cannot build Christ into us, He cannot reveal Christ to us. There is something wrong and real fellowship cannot overlook that—not real fellowship. Although the Holy Spirit loves us, He wants to fellowship, come alongside, strengthen us, He has to send us a rebuke letter in order to open fellowship with us. Have you ever received a rebuke letter from the Holy Spirit?

I believe as truly as Paul agonized, the Holy Spirit agonizes. His calling is to dwell in you, form Christ in you, and when He is grieved and stifled and resisted and disobeyed, when He is quenched and laying silent inside, He is an agony and a groaning and an intercession that the will of God will be done in your life. Here is the mystery of mysteries. On the one hand, our God is absolutely complacent because He knows the end from the beginning. It is all finished and the victory is won; yet at the same time He can be immanent in us striving, struggling, crying, grieving over us. Do you think the Holy Spirit does that? Do you think He says, "Well, I will just wait around; time for a little vacation anyway"? No, not the Holy Spirit. This is why Paul's letter is an illustration of the Holy Spirit's fellowship with us.

REPENTANCE RESTORED FELLOWSHIP

Then Paul shares the good outcome in II Corinthians 7:6-10: "But God, who comforts the depressed (meaning him), comforted us (strengthened us) by the coming of Titus; and not only by his coming, but also by the comfort with which he was comforted in you, as he reported to us your longing, your mourning, your zeal for me; so that I rejoiced even more. For though I caused you sorrow by my letter, I do not regret it; though I did regret it—for I see that that letter caused you sorrow, though only for a while—I now rejoice, not that you were made sorrowful, but that you were made sorrowful to the point of repentance; for you were made sorrowful according to the will of God in order that you might not suffer loss in anything through us. For the sorrow that is according to the will of God, produces a repentance without regret, leading to salvation, but the sorrow of the world produces death."

Paul says, "I am comforted, I am exuberant. I rejoice because the letter brought repentance and opened up our relationship again. Now we can fellowship brother to brother, we can share Christ with one another, and the blockage is gone because you repented." Brothers and sisters, the Holy Spirit wants to fellowship with us but most of the time He has got to come and say, "Repent." This is the door many times into our fellowship with Him: "Lay that down. I will not talk to you until you lay that down." He will agonize and He will wait until that moment when we repent.

Let's look at a few passages on repentance. In Acts 11:18, when the disciples heard what happened in Cornelius' house, they said, "They have received the repentance that leads to life." Repentance always leads to life. In our fellowship with the Holy Spirit, repentance, so often, is the way into life.

In a teenage meeting this is so apparent. The sweetest fellowship that I know is the fellowship of the teenagers when they have repented and their hearts are clear with God. They sing all night, they are in the sweetest fellowship, they are broken, they love one another, they love the Lord, they openly confess. It is such a wonderful thing to see what happens when they repent: "There He is right there. I thought He had gone far away but He is right there." It is the sweetest fellowship. It is precious because the result of repentance is fellowship.

There is an illustration in II Timothy 2:24. It is a word given by Paul to Timothy about how to deal with quarrelsome men. "The Lord's bond-servant must not be quarrelsome, but be kind to all, able to teach, patient when wronged, with gentleness correcting those who are in opposition, if perhaps God may grant them repentance leading to the knowledge of the truth."

We have a problem. Sometimes, external, outward doctrines prevent us from knowing the revealed truth. Sometimes, we understand things wrongly and need repentance to see the truth. These men had some doctrines that were wrong and Timothy is told to go and patiently explain to them the truth and then pray that ay grant them the repentance that will lead them to the truth. There are people who get involved in cults and in wrong teaching and then they come into fellowship among you, but something is wrong. Until they repent of the wrong teaching and renounce it, they do not come into the light. It is repentance that leads us to truth. When we have held some idea of the Holy Spirit that is wrong, it is not up to us to say, "Well, let's just move on." No; "I repent, precious, loving God, Holy Spirit for my wrong understanding of who

You are. I have come to see You now as my Lord, as my God," There is life right there. Repentance is the doorway.

We see the entreating Holy Spirit and we see the Lord, the risen Lord Himself, in Revelation 2 and 3. In five out of seven churches, He is saying, "Please, do you want to fellowship with Me? Repent, repent, repent; change your mind, change your direction. Why are you holding on to Jezebel and outward things? Throw her out. Why are you holding on to the teachings of Balaam and the Nicolaitans? Throw those out. Why are you holding on to anything except Me? Throw it out. Why do you think you are rich and increased with goods? Throw that stuff out; buy from Me; repent." What He wants is fellowship. He wants resurrection ground, the power, and the grace to overcome in our lives but if we do not repent, if we are too spiritual or deceived to repent, there is not going to be much progress in our lives. We stifle this free fellowship. We take fellowship with the Holy Spirit lightly. He demands honesty and a clear conscience and repentance.

There is a cross in repentance, but every time we do something like that, we find ourselves closer to the Lord than before. So, Paul's fellowship by letter is a good illustration of how the Holy Spirit yearns to fellowship with us if we just listen when He speaks. Don't harden your heart; then we will have fellowship with Him and He builds Christ into our lives.

THE HOLY SPIRIT WRITES CHRIST ON OUR HEARTS

As we continue on in II Corinthians 3 and 4, we see the necessary transition from an outward ministry of the word to an inward understanding of the nature of the new covenant. Paul talks about things that we have often heard about. In chapter 3:3, he says, "Being manifested that you are a letter of Christ, cared for by us, written not with ink, but with the Spirit of the living God, not on tables of stone, but on tables of human hearts."

How does the Spirit minister to us? He writes Christ on our hearts. When we read the word of God, He does not just give us outward knowledge. It is not in outward knowledge that we find life, but it is in what the Spirit writes on our hearts. These are the indelible things. They enable us to know God. In the new covenant, the law is written in your heart. The new covenant ministry is primarily an internal ministry. So it is not just a question of reading the word externally, la de da. It is a question of a fellowship where Spirit and life come to us as He makes the logos rhema. The word, the logos, becomes rhema as we fellowship with the Spirit which is life.

Paul makes a contrast here in verse 7 with the old covenant ministration where he says, "But if the ministry of death, in letters engraved on stones, came with glory..."; and he begins to talk about the old. Here is the contrast, that the old covenant was written on stones; it was outward, external, and when they read it, there was a veil. Then he says in II Corinthians 3:14–15, "But their minds were hardened; for until this very day at the reading of the old covenant the same veil remains unlifted, because it is removed in Christ. But to this day whenever Moses is read, a veil lies over their hearts."

THE VEIL

A Veil Over the Heart

When these lovers of God would read the law, the torah, there was a veil upon their hearts. Maybe it was the veil of tradition because they were reading through eyes of tradition. Or maybe it was just the veil of human reason, as they would try and reason with it. Any time anyone understands something with their mind, they impede the possibility of revelation: "I know this." Well, you will not get any revelation then. The veil among the Jews in Paul's day existed primarily for two reasons. An understanding of the spirit of the word of God comes only by revelation, and the key to the interpretation of the Law lay in seeing the Messiah throughout it.

Then Paul says in verse 16, "But whenever [it] turns to the Lord, the veil is taken away." That is what it literally says in the Greek. The New American Standard says, "Whenever a person turns to the Lord"; but it actually says, "Whenever it turns to the Lord," meaning the heart. "But when the heart turns to the Lord, the veil is taken away." He is testifying of this: "My heart turned to the Lord Jesus and then I read the same law and there was no veil. Now I look at the word of God and I see Jesus. Look, He is in Deuteronomy; look, He is in Genesis because my eyes have been opened and the Holy Spirit is able to reveal things. Now it is life when I am reading and there is no veil because I have turned to the Lord."

It was the same precious word, but it was veiled because they did not have Christ as the key nor the quickening and the illumining of the Holy Spirit. But because we have turned to the Lord, the Holy Spirit is our Revealer. This is what he means in verse 17; "Now the Lord is Spirit, and where the Spirit of the Lord is, there is liberty." It is not talking about liberty to dance or worship but a freedom to understand the word of God. When the Spirit is the Lord, when you come to the Lord and turn your heart to the Lord and say, "Lord, show me, reveal Your word to me," then there is liberty. Suddenly, you understand and you see Jesus.

A Veil Over the Eyes

In verse 18 it says, "But we all, with unveiled face beholding as in a mirror the glory of the Lord, are being transformed into the same image from glory to glory, just as from the Lord, the Spirit." The Spirit has a reason for revealing Jesus in the word. While you are looking at it, it transforms you a little bit into the same image that you see by revelation. Something is written into your heart. This is the ministry of the Holy Spirit. He comes and communes with us. There is a cross in it. We have to allow no veil. It is strange to say, but there are Christians who read the Scriptures with a veil over their eyes. They are not reading in dependence upon the Lord; they are just reading with their external reasoning. Now what does a Jew or a Christian receive with his external understanding? A letter—a letter that kills. But what if you come depending upon the Lord? You say, "Lord, take the veil off my eyes, let me see Jesus." When you open the word, something more is going on because the Holy Spirit is communing through this word. So you see, very practically, there is a veil here that needs to be taken away and then you see Christ and He builds Christ into you. So there must be a death, a removal of the old as it were, and then resurrecting life in Christ as you read the word.

When young people begin to get exercised about serving the Lord, they always come up with this issue: "How do you study the word of God in a living way?" So I tell them that every morning when you get up, there is just a little ice on the lake. Somehow it got a little bit below freezing in your heart while you were sleeping. The young people want to love God, but when they get up in the morning and look at the Bible, they say, "This thing is pretty musty. It is just letter to me. I don't know. The last time I tried this it didn't work; I don't know." There comes in a little resistance, a little doubt, there is a little veil, a little something there. So I say to them: "You just go to the Lord and say, 'Lord, I just break the ice right now. By Your Spirit speak to me, show me Jesus.'" Then open the word of God and you will see something. There has got to be a little something on our part of laying aside. If you just go to the Bible with your usual brain power, when you get through with your Bible study, you do not even remember what you've read.

A Veil Over the Gospel

Paul also says in II Corinthians chapter 4 that a veil also covers up the gospel. He says, "I preached the gospel of Jesus Christ, but you know, the enemy puts a veil over the gospel so the people cannot see. But there is a God who says 'Let there be light,' and when He shines into a person's heart with revelation, then they see." As he says in verse 6: "For God, who said, 'Light shall shine out of darkness,' is the One who has shone in our hearts to give the light of the knowledge of the glory of God in the face of Christ." When somebody hears the gospel and the Holy Spirit shines in their heart, they see that Jesus is God. That is always the issue. The Lord Jesus is a great man; yes, He is a good teacher, but to see Jesus as God, that veil of the enemy has to be taken off the eyes. That is why when we preach the gospel, there is some warfare.

Paul goes on to say, "Now we have this treasure in earthen vessels and when I am preaching the gospel, I am preaching the gospel

of Christ as His servant, for Jesus' sake.
Sometimes, when I am preaching the gospel and
the gospel is veiled, God says, 'I am going to
show them My glorious gospel through you' and
He breaks Paul. In one sense, Paul becomes a
living letter and in Paul's broken life people see
Jesus. That is why it is in that context. There is a
veil. The enemy would have us be veiled from
the gospel but if you have Jesus in your heart, if
He is dwelling there by the work of the Holy
Spirit, if you have Jesus with you as you preach
the gospel, then the Lord can break you and
people will see treasure. They say, "How come
he loves us so much? We just rejected the gospel
and here he is, loving us. What is going on here?"
They see something in the servant of God. So
Paul says, "The Lord, in one sense, takes me
around the block. He uses me to preach, then
people persecute or stone me and notice: 'You
know what? He is not acting the way most
people do when you stone them. He has forgiven
us, he is praying for us, he is saying, 'Save them,
Jesus.'"

I remember one time when I was out on the
street in Manhattan and I was with this famous

evangelist. He was working the streets preaching the gospel and I was walking along with him, handing out tracts and preaching. A drunk guy came up to this brother with a knife in his hand, and he said, "I am going to cut you to ribbons." This brother said, "All one thousand pieces are going to love you because Jesus died for your sins." That man fell down and got saved right there. This is the ministry of the Holy Spirit in our lives.

THE UNDERMINING OF AUTHORITY

There is one last illustration of the fellowship of the Holy Spirit that we have time to note in II Corinthians. It begins in chapter 10, where Paul deals with the challenge to his apostolic authority. The Corinthians, as we read earlier in II Corinthians 10:7, looked at things from an external point of view and had begun to measure the various apostles. Now mind you, the men that Paul is responding to are not Peter, or Apollos, not those servants of God. They were some men who stood up and self-proclaimed themselves apostles. Nobody set them up; they set themselves up. Maybe they were from some rhetorical school; maybe they had a lot of flare, maybe they had a Cadillac; we don't know. But what they basically were doing was undermining Paul's authority as an apostle there in Corinth.

They were challenging him. "For they say, 'His letters are weighty and strong, but his personal presence is unimpressive, and his speech contemptible'" (v. 10). In effect they were saying, "Paul has got a lot of bluff when he sends those tough letters, but he is not such a big dude. He has a big nose, a squeaky voice, he's short, not at all what we would call a man of God, a man of faith and power." Paul says, "Why do you look at the outward?" Then, as if provoked to share his outward credentials, he begins to list some in II Corinthians 12:11-13: "I have become foolish; you yourselves compelled me. Actually I should have been commended by you, for in no respect was I inferior to the most eminent apostles, even though I am a nobody. The signs of a true apostle were performed among you with all perseverance, by signs and wonders and miracles. For in what respect were you treated as inferior to the rest of the churches, except that I myself did not become a burden to you? Forgive me this wrong!"

He begins to share outward evidences, although he says in chapter 10:12: "For we are not bold to class or compare ourselves with some of those who commend themselves; for when they measure themselves by themselves, and compare themselves with themselves, they are without understanding." He says, "Okay, let's compare. Now who preaches better? Who uses better Greek?" Paul says, "I am not even going to get into that measurement match." Then he said, "But something is driving me here and I will let you know what it is. I have a jealous love for you and I, actually, don't care what you think of me. I have a jealous love for you. That is my credential. Do you know what my problem is? I have tried to keep you as a chaste virgin for the Bridegroom and you are chasing after every outward thing. Where is your discernment? If another spirit comes along or another gospel, you say, 'Oh, that sounds great, it is logical, plausible, emotional.'" He says, "I am telling you the flat out truth: 'These men are false apostles and from the enemy.'"

Listen to what he says there in chapter 11:13: "For such men are false apostles, deceitful workers, disguising themselves as apostles of Christ. And no wonder, for even Satan disguises himself as an angel of light." "Don't you have any inward life? Don't you know Jesus? How can you listen to them and think that is Jesus? How is the church going to survive if you cannot recognize the Spirit of your Head, the Lord Jesus? When somebody comes along and flaunts a ministry with power that has people doing things and acting like monkeys, don't you see the contrast with the character of Jesus? Don't you know that He always has respect for human beings? He never treated anybody like an animal. Where are your sensibilities? Where is your discernment, church? What is the matter with you, don't you know Jesus? Listen, you have been born again by Jesus and the Holy Spirit has been working in you. You know the word of God; don't you know Jesus yet? Satan is the angel of light and so his false apostles will look good or do something good or powerful."

Americans are so naïve. All over the world, there are hundreds of religious groups with people speaking in tongues and performing miracles and all that, but that is not necessarily a sign of authenticity. Here is the sign of authenticity: Does somebody look like Christ? Are they ministering like Christ with that same deference, humility, love, or is it arrogance, self-exalting? Is it a show, or does he take somebody aside and heal them in secret saying, "Now, don't tell anybody"? What is the character of that ministry? That is how we recognize something legitimate. Paul says, "Why are you dealing with these outward things? Look inside." Paul is furious; so furious that he says, "All right, you want a list? You think they are apostles; I am more than they are. I am a Hebrew of the Hebrews, I am the best of the Pharisees, I have been in more places, in more shipwrecks, I have had more stonings, more floggings and have been shipwrecked in the sea. You compare them with my list

Why is Paul doing this seemingly foolish thing? It is because the Corinthians should be ashamed of themselves. They are violating something so deep. Do you know what it is? Paul is their spiritual father and they are measuring their father. How dare they do that! It is a violation of fellowship. It is not that anyone is above making sure that they are following Christ. But Paul says, "You know, I am your father. I am not out to control you or use you like these other people do. They get money from you. I don't get money from you. I am not out to use you, I am out to help you. I am your father; don't you see it? What is apostleship? I stay up all night worrying about you. That's apostleship; that's love. How can you use me and now throw me out?" They say, "We want a more modern version." There is a violation of fellowship there. Paul's heart was inflamed to tell the truth, even though it made him look like a fool. He even tells on himself: "I can only really boast of my foolishness. When I got saved in Damascus, I preached the gospel a few days and had to be lowered down in a basket over the wall to escape. How foolish did I look. You see, I am nothing if you want to look at that kind of stuff. But maybe if you look at my heart you will see my heart is open to you. I am not holding anything back. And I would give you my life, indeed, I have, just to see you grow. What is wrong with you?"

CHECK THE ANOINTING WITHIN

Then finally, Paul shares something in chapter 13 that really is an issue. Why are the Corinthians so head-strong, so outward in their view of things? Could it be that they had never had a revelation of the fact that Christ loved them and that there was an indwelling Holy Spirit, that they knew more of the wind than the breath? You will notice in II Corinthians 13:5 it says, "Test yourselves to see if you are in the faith; examine yourselves! Or do you not recognize this about yourselves, that Jesus Christ is in you—unless indeed you fail the test?" What is he saying to them? We know this is a chronic problem because in I Corinthians 3:16 where he is talking about the church corporately and the way the church corporately should be built, he says, "Do you not know that you are a temple of God and that the Spirit of God dwells in you?"

They probably would have said: "Of course, we know that. You told us that when you were here." Paul was saying, "Now wait a minute, I know you know the doctrine but do you really know that the Holy Spirit dwells in you? Do you know that you are a living organism and the Holy Spirit is in you and in you and in you? Are you going to build garbage on one another? Are you going to build foolishly on one another? Don't you realize that you are the temple of the living God, that God the Holy Spirit lives in you? You need to learn to treat one another with respect. No wonder so many of you are sick when you come to the Lord's table because you do not see the Holy Spirit in one another. Do you know the Holy Spirit lives in all of you?"

Brothers and sisters, do we know that? Do we see it as a revelation? Look what he says in chapter 6:19-20 when he makes a personal reference concerning immorality: "Or do you not know that your body is a temple of the Holy Spirit who is in you, whom you have from God, and that you are not your own? For you have been bought with a price: therefore glorify God in your body." How can a Christian who knows he is the temple of the Holy Spirit commit immorality? Don't you think that they would feel such pressure inside from the grieving Holy Spirit? Don't you think they would be at all spooked by the fact that God is going with you over there? But if you do not see that by revelation then we can act carelessly, we can say anything, do anything; who cares? God is not looking. I beg your pardon. He is living inside of you and if we saw that revelation, we would start seeing things a lot differently.

Going back to their relationship with Paul, if they saw that the Spirit was in Paul and in them, they would honor him and respect him for the Christ that they saw in him. Paul is not really tooting his own horn, neither is he, as some commentaries say, defending his apostleship. He is trying to correct, in the fellowship of the Holy Spirit, an outward view of apostleship that would prevent the church from going on through history on a proper course. He just wanted them to see that an apostle like Peter or Apollos is a man who is filled with the nature of Christ and also the Spirit of God. We also should not be taken in by outward things. Check that anointing within you. Every Christian has this intuitive anointing that this is right or this is wrong. Why aren't you checking it? Why are you so overwhelmed by the hot wind of some ministry?

Listen inside; if something is going on inside, check.

THE CHARACTER OF CHRIST FORMED

So we have seen that the communion of the Holy Spirit within is absolutely essential for us to be the testimony of the Lord. We can have all the power of the Holy Spirit but if we do not have the character of Christ, we will go off the rails into deception in these last days. There will be deceiving spirits all over the place that will mock, imitate, and counterfeit everything that God really is. We need the anointing inside, we need brothers in leadership who have the character of Christ, we need to listen to them, we need to know the government of God in prayer because, sometimes, when the enemy assails, it is not flesh and blood. In II Corinthians 10, Paul saw that this apostolic challenge was not a flesh and blood challenge anyway. It was something vaunting itself up against the knowledge of Christ in the life of these Corinthians, and Paul said, "I stand with the Holy Spirit who stands for the Lord being revealed and I say that these men will be toppled down and disciplined as soon as your obedience is complete."

I believe in these last days we need to move by an anointing within that knows the life of the Lord. We need to come to the place where we will understand His will because we know Him and not just because we read something or somebody told us this is the will of God. If you know the Lord well enough, you will understand what He wants and what His will is. We need to have this internal life of Christ by the Spirit. That is our only hope. For sure, the wind of the Holy Spirit will blow. I hope He blows where I live and where you live and He does mighty things. But oh, I pray for men and women of character and with the faith and strength to stand up and say, "This is right and this is wrong," and to have the kind of discernment to test reality among us in the last days.

The communion of the Holy Spirit can be a reality to us if we will let the Holy Spirit reveal Christ to us and then work it into our lives, to bring the cross to us, and bring us through to resurrection ground like Paul. As he says in II

Corinthians 4:7, "But we have this treasure in earthen vessels, that the surpassing greatness of the power may be of God and not from ourselves." May the Lord deal with us in such a way that He can truly build Christ-likeness into us. May we find, even though we are just earthen vessels, that there is a treasure among us and among the saints. May we fellowship with the Holy Spirit and let this treasure increase in manifestation in our lives. I think there will come a day, perhaps pretty soon, where believers will become so sated with every kind of wind, power, menagerie, and show that the saints will come back around and say, "Please, show us somebody with the character of Christ." Will you be ready? Can you show them the truth and the liberty that is in Christ Jesus? You can show Him because you are abiding in the grace of Jesus Christ and the love of God and the fellowship of the Holy Spirit. This is indeed our benediction. The Holy Spirit longs that we live in the reality of these things. God our Father has even allowed us to come together in these days to be reminded of this. There is a place where we can dwell, a hiding place in these last days, a house that the Father has prepared, a place of blessing and a place of life, a place of spiritual power, a place of His wonderful presence. It is the place marked by the grace of our Lord Jesus Christ, the love of God, and the fellowship of the Holy Spirit. May that be ours now and forever more.

Let us pray:

We want to worship You, our loving God, because You do faithfully, day by day, energetically work within us, revealing Christ to us, convincing us that Christ is all, stripping from us our alliances, producing life, resurrection life, life that cannot be defeated, life that knows the truth and the way.

We give all glory to Jesus Christ who opened us up to this whole inner reality. That we can walk in our various different cities and towns and on our various different jobs, and yet be walking with Him and talking with Him because we live in a house without geography. We abide in a Christ who is with us all the time and we have a communion of a faithful Holy Spirit, servant of the cross and the resurrection, to bring us through, guaranteed, into eternal life in experience.

We pray that the ministration of the Father, Son and Holy Spirit will be worked out in our days in such a way that these matters will no longer just be doctrines but true reality for us. We want to be such spiritual men as Paul who begin to understand how to abide by looking not at things that are seen but at unseen. We thank You for the precious treasure we have in Christ.

Sometimes, in our outward view, we have even doubted the value of that treasure. Forgive us, Lord. We repent. We have the greatest treasure of all and if you have stripped away from us some of the earthen treasures in order that we may gain Christ, then we count those things but dung and thank You that we have gained Christ and more of Him. And so we forget the things that are behind and we press toward the goal of the high calling of God in Christ Jesus. We thank you for this comforting fortification of the Holy Spirit who runs with us and strengthens us in this race that You have set for us.

O Lord, thank You for Your blessings. Do seal Your word, use it for Your own glory. We pray in Jesus' name. Amen.

Other Books Printed By
Christian Testimony Ministry

SPEAKER	TITLE
DANA CONGDON	MARRIAGE, SINGLENESS, AND THE WILL OF GOD
	RECOVERY & RESTORATION
	THE HOLY SPIRIT
	HEBREWS
A.J. FLACK	TENT OF HIS SPLENDOUR
STEPHEN KAUNG	ACTS
	BE YE THEREFORE PERFECT
	CALLED OUT UNTO CHRIST
	CALLED TO THE FELLOWSHIP OF GOD'S SON
	DIVINE LIFE AND ORDER
	FOR ME TO LIVE IS CHRIST
	GLORIOUS LIBERTY OF THE CHILDREN OF GOD
	GOD'S PURPOSE FOR THE FAMILY
	I WILL BUILD MY CHURCH
	MEDITATIONS ON THE KINGDOM
	RECOVERY
	SPIRITUAL EXERCISE
	SPIRITUAL LIFE (II CORINTHIANS SERIES)
	TEACH US TO PRAY
	THE CROSS
	THE FULNESS OF CHRIST—IN THE BOOK OF REVELATION
	THE HEADSHIP OF CHRIST
	THE KINGDOM AND THE CHURCH
	THE KINGDOM OF GOD
	THE LAST CALL TO THE CHURCHES, THE CALL TO OVERCOME
	THE LIFE OF OUR LORD JESUS
	THE LIFE OF THE CHURCH, THE BODY OF CHRIST
	THE LORD'S TABLE
	TWO GUIDEPOSTS FOR INHERITING THE KINGDOM
	VISION OF CHRIST (REVELATION)
	WHO ARE WE?

WHY DO WE SO GATHER?
WORSHIP

LANCE LAMBERT   CALLED UNTO HIS ETERNAL GLORY
                      GOD'S ETERNAL PURPOSE
                      IN THE DAY OF THY POWER
                      JACOB I HAVE LOVED
                      LIVING FAITH
                      LESSONS FROM THE LIFE OF MOSES
                      LOVE DIVINE
                      MY HOUSE SHALL BE A HOUSE OF PRAYER
                      PREPARATION FOR THE COMING OF THE LORD
                      REIGNING WITH CHRIST
                      SPIRITUAL CHARACTER
                      THE GOSPEL OF THE KINGDOM
                      THE IMPORTANCE OF COVERING
                      THE LAST DAYS AND GOD'S PRIORITIES
                      THE PRIZE
                      THE SUPREMACY OF JESUS CHRIST
                      THINE IS THE POWER!
                      THOU ART MINE

T. AUSTIN-SPARKS   THE LORD'S TESTIMONY AND THE WORLD NEED

HARVEY CEDARS CONFERENCE

STEPHEN KAUNG   HEAVENLY VISION
                      SPIRITUAL RESPONSIBILITY

CONGDON, HILE, KAUNG SPIRITUAL MINISTRY
                      SPIRITUAL AUTHORITY
                      SPIRITUAL HOUSE
                      SPIRITUAL SUBMISSION

STEPHEN KAUNG   SPIRITUAL KNOWLEDGE
                      SPIRITUAL POWER
                      SPIRITUAL REALITY
                      SPIRITUAL VALUE
                      SPIRITUAL BLESSING
                      SPIRITUAL DISCERNMENT

www.ingramcontent.com/pod-product-compliance
Lightning Source LLC
Chambersburg PA
CBHW051041030426
42339CB00006B/142